AF324881

John Beech

BRIDGED FIELD
Found-Photo Drawings

Foreword by Alexander Nagel

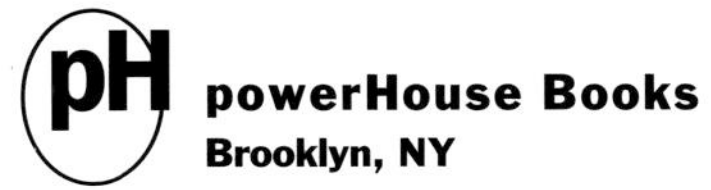

John Beech's Found-Photo Drawings
or, How to Live

Alexander Nagel

The world provides plenty of discarded photographs that can be picked up in junk shops. Still. They tend to be somewhat old, because of changing technologies, but also because any dumping usually comes after a lag. But they are cheap, not quite vintage. To paint or draw on these photos is to extend and articulate a relation defined by fairly clear parameters. I take the whole process as a guide to living.

John Beech doesn't select for the best photos. ("In fact, the really good ones I don't paint on.") He chooses the ones that have an interesting texture. That's his word, and I take it to mean it has an inviting imperfection, that it has tooth, so to speak, that it might respond well to an intervention. *As you move through the world, don't just get to places. Look at what is there—but not as an aesthetic picture. Look at it, seeing it as something that is good and imperfect and might need you to act in it.*

If you turn this page and the one beneath it, you'll uncover the first work reproduced in this book. You will notice that the artist acknowledges the photo not just as an image but as an object. One corner of the photographic print has been ripped, and the corner opposite has been folded and then flattened again. The painting activity has in fact brought these features into relief. Strokes of paint mount towards the torn corner but then leave it clear, a counter-pressure to the metal beam that meets it. At the other corner, a previous layer of paint, wiped away, has caught on the ridge of the once-folded paper, yielding a line made by no one. It looks like a crack, something showing through what now appears to be marble or glass. *Don't just look at the thing but at the ground of the thing. Don't view people as resolved figures; see them against their ground and interact with their ground. Then you will see them differently.*

Before turning this page, go to pages 94–95 and look at both images on the spread.

The two approaches are so different it is as if they are not part of the same project. But they are. We need to have both approaches.

Left side
Negation would be the wrong word, but a certain disregard is necessary to the approach. The photo is not an inspiration, but it does get used. It is turned to its side and only its most crudely identifiable feature, a grey grid of sorts, is set up. Then it is disregarded. The white splotch that has accumulated observes no distinction between the printed part of the photo and the white border. It has no relation to the photographic information, not even a contrasting one, not even a negating one. The paint avoids the look of having been applied as if something was meant to be done with it, and it is even farther from the idea that it is a form of geomancy, that the earth or some other power guided the brush. The green paint below is scraped remnants from some other activity, activity possibly meant for some other surface, as if this were the newspaper protecting the floor. What does it mean to work on something while not noticing it? What space do you have to be in to achieve this disregard? *There are times when you don't need to get along and you don't need to go against the grain. You use the world, but you don't let it determine your actions, nor do you insist on self-determination. And yet you act.*

Right side

If you are like me, you did not at first disentangle the added lines from the photographic information here. You saw lines enjoying a freedom that would merely fling wide but for a measure of elasticity that keeps them in relation to one another. This is dancing that dispenses with mere rhythm. You did not at first see a chair but were imagining unheard-of musical instruments. But then things start to settle out, the upended chair is distinguished, seen to be twirled and gently caught, upside-down but still poised, tethered by fluid but firm lines. Momentarily, we imagine that this is clever and start to become clever ourselves. We note that the lines are very close in thickness and tone and swoop to the curves of the chair, and—look!—even the white streaks of paper left in the wake of the faster strokes rhyme with the sliding reflections on the limbs of the chair. But that is to take a very static approach. Mimicry begins by fixing the object, whereas this work begins by upending the thing, releasing it from its usual definition and function. And now we have the result before us, offering us a new configuration that is both stable and unstable. *If you fix the thing you cannot enter into relation to it. Defamiliarize it so that you can dance with it.*

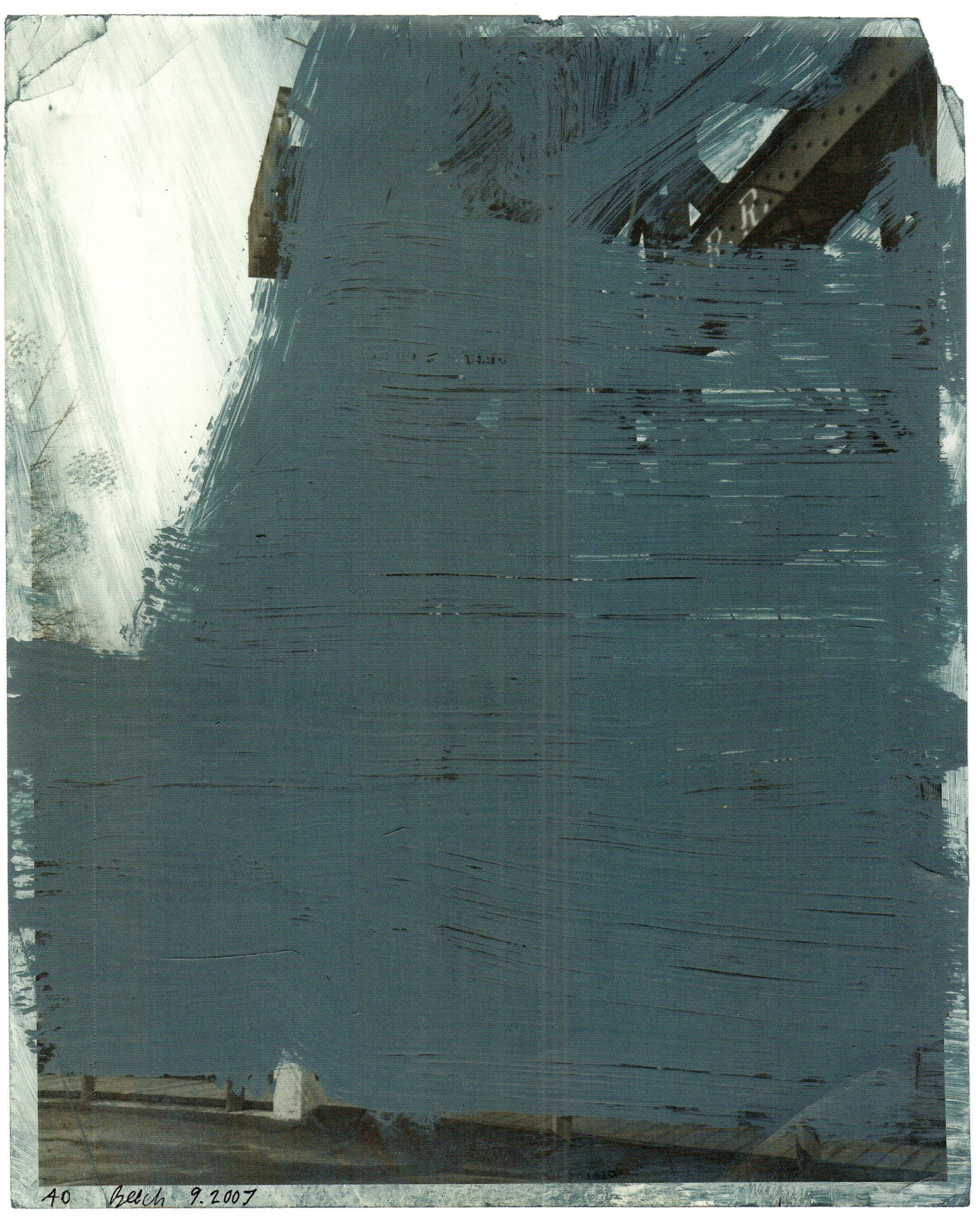
40   Belch   9.2007

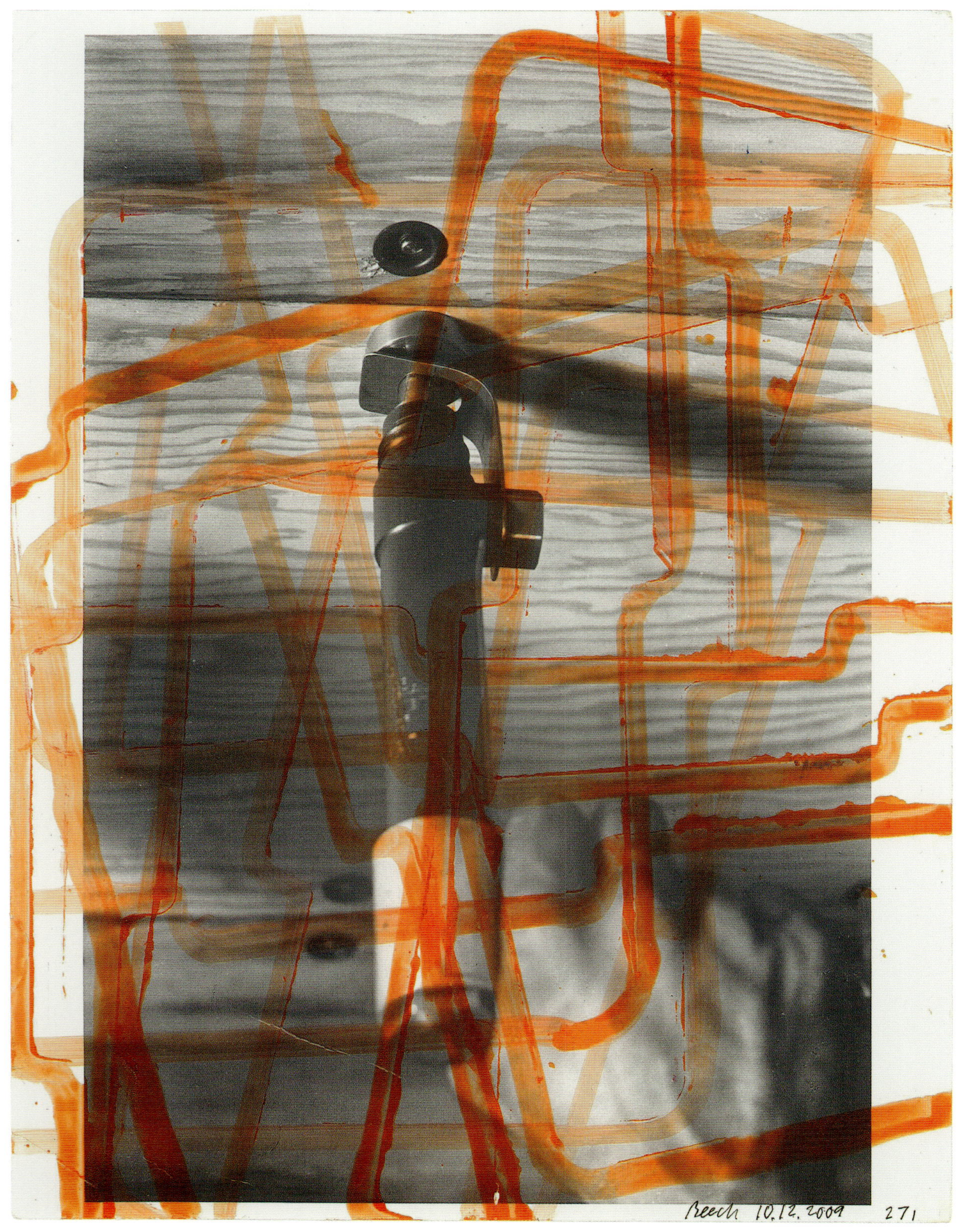

Beech 10.12.2009   271

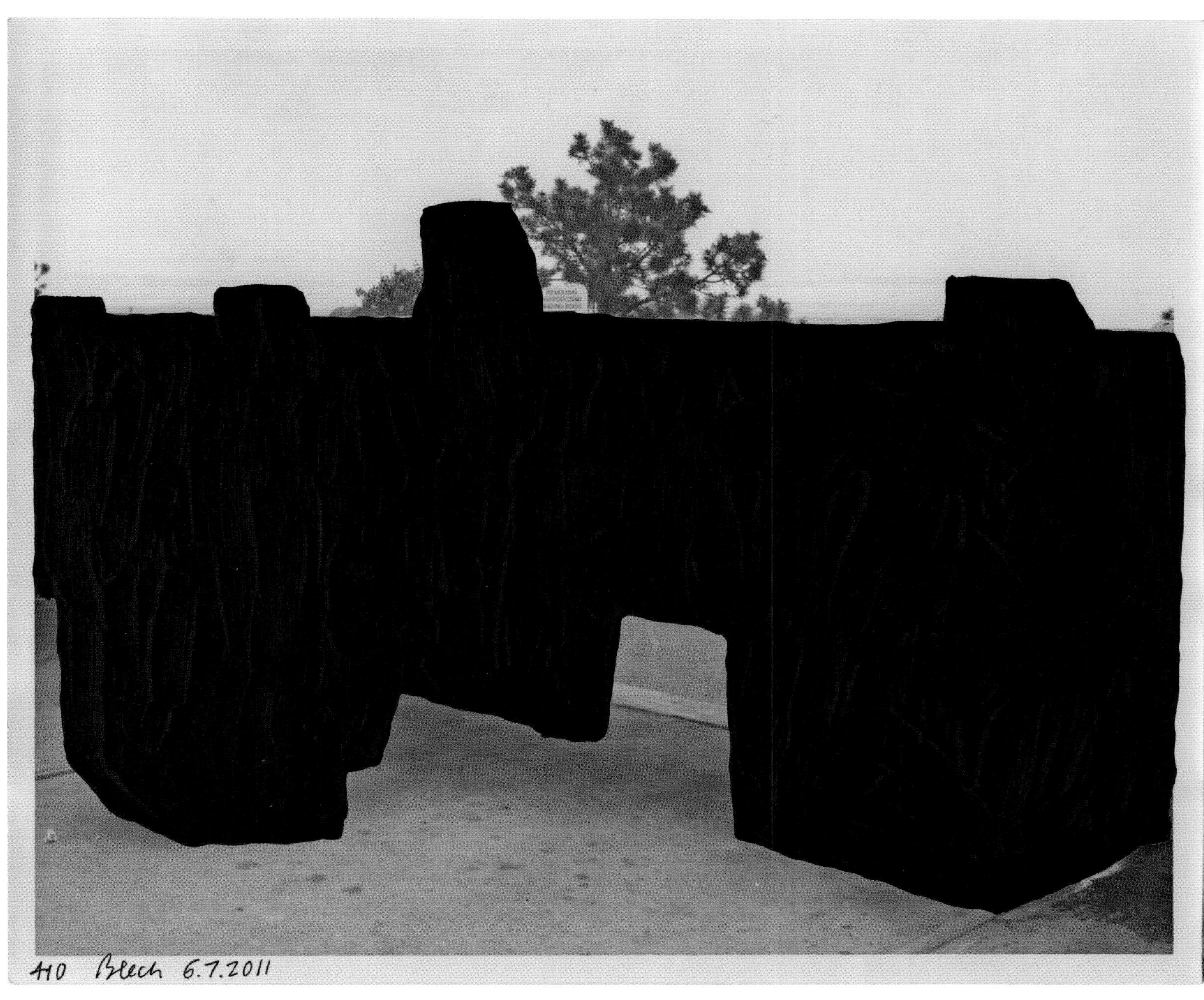

410 Blech 6.7.2011

47

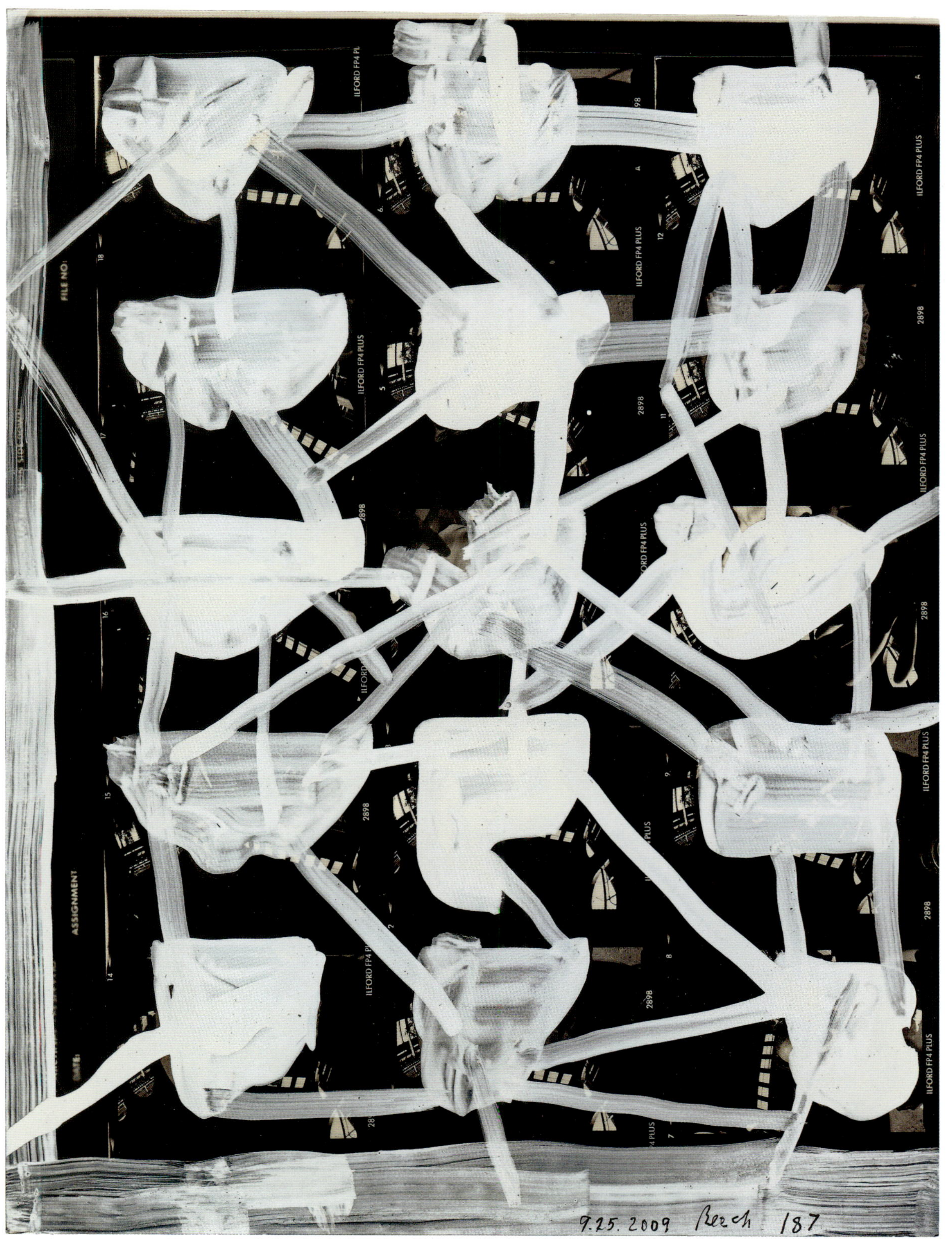

9.25.2009 Berch 187

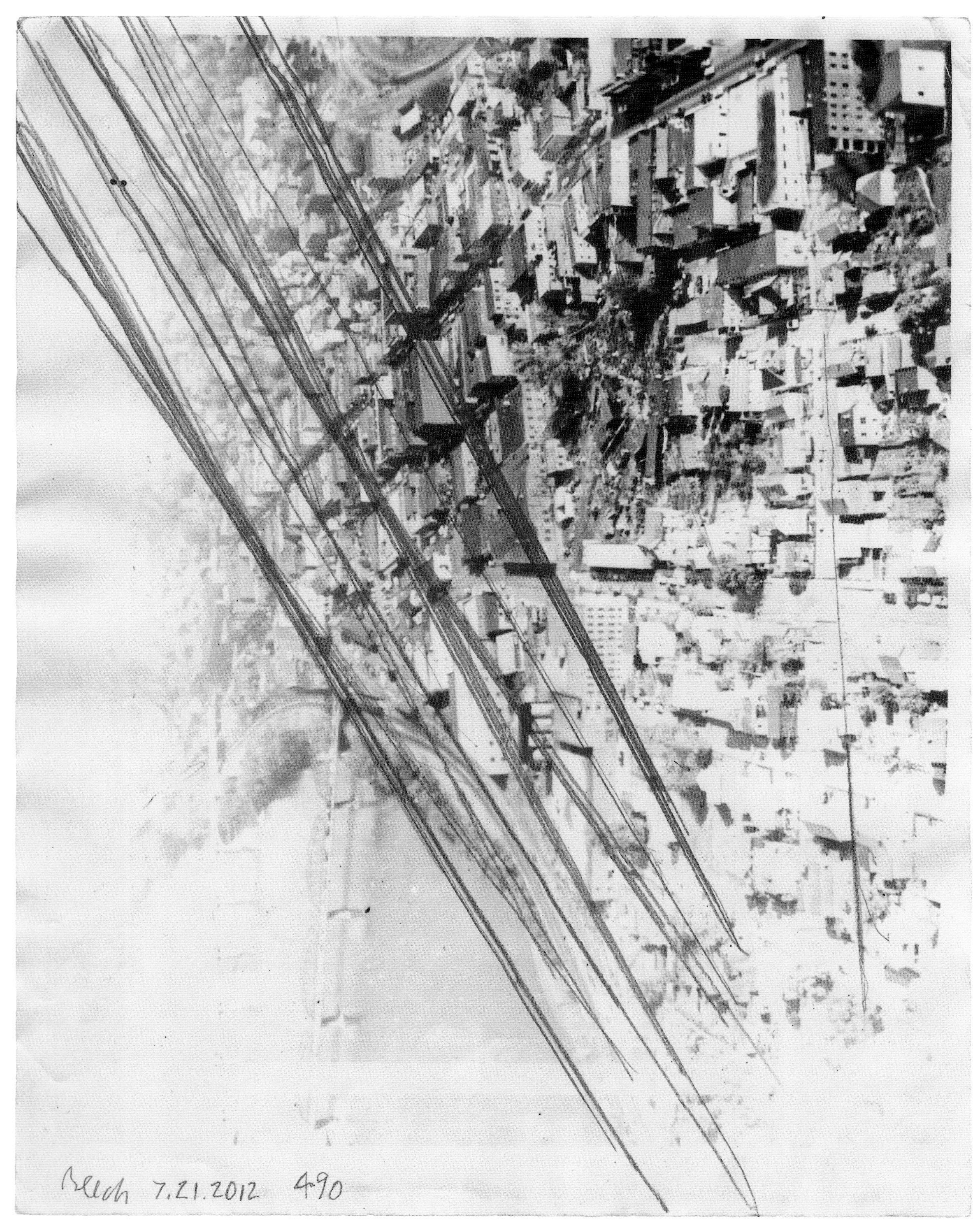

Beech 7.21.2012 490

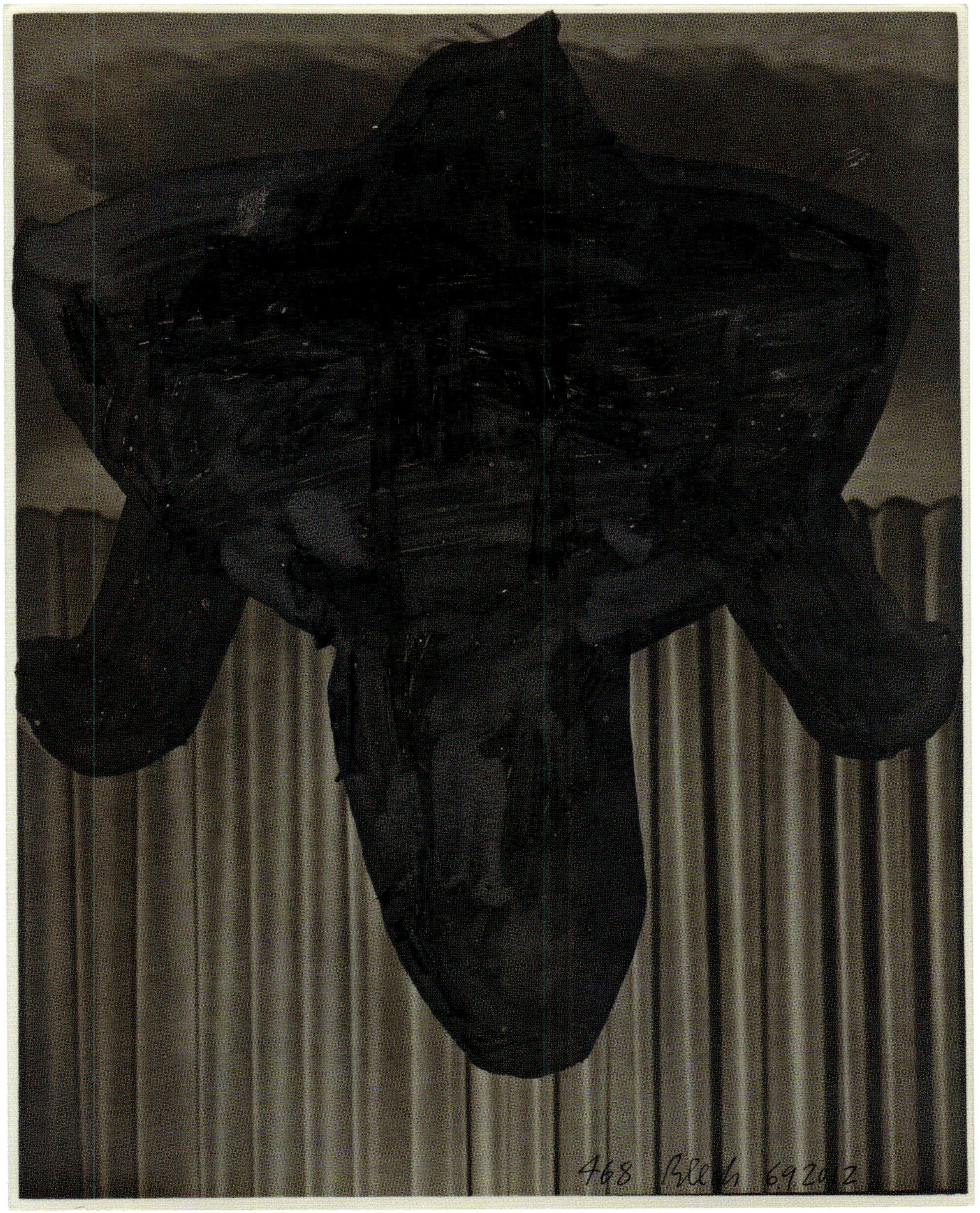

468 Bloch 6.9.2012

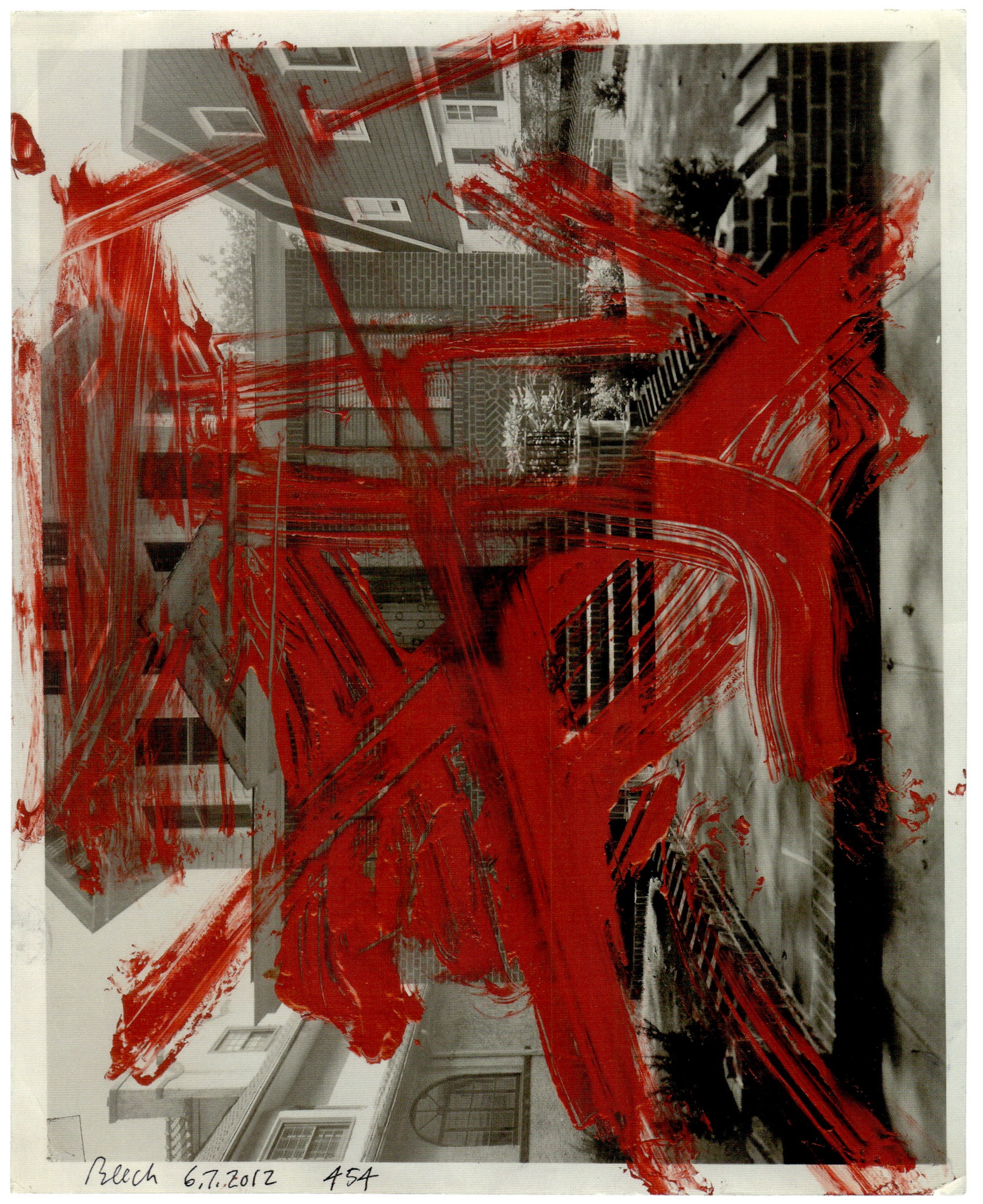

Blech 6.7.2012   454

10.17.2009
281
Blech
10.18.2009

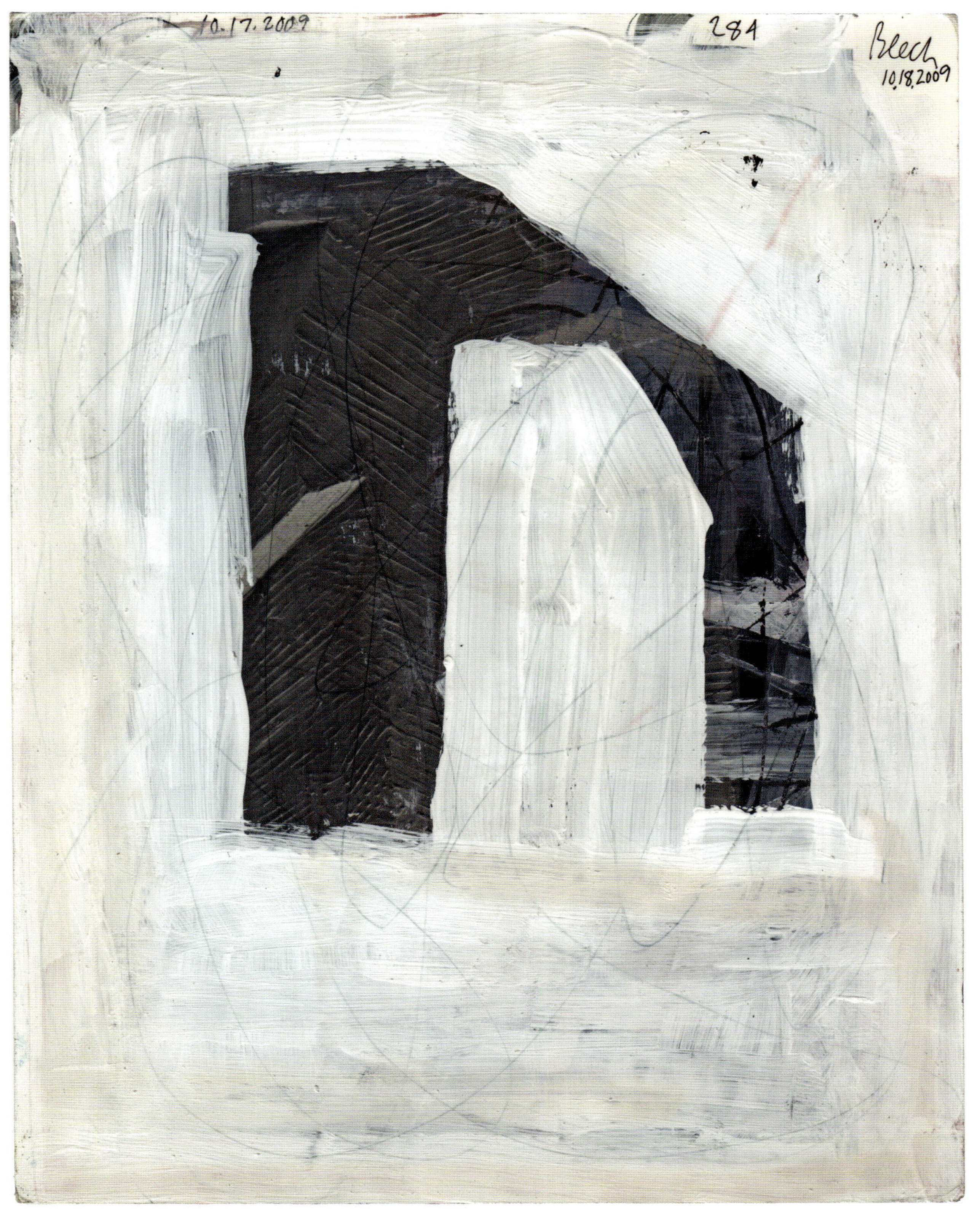

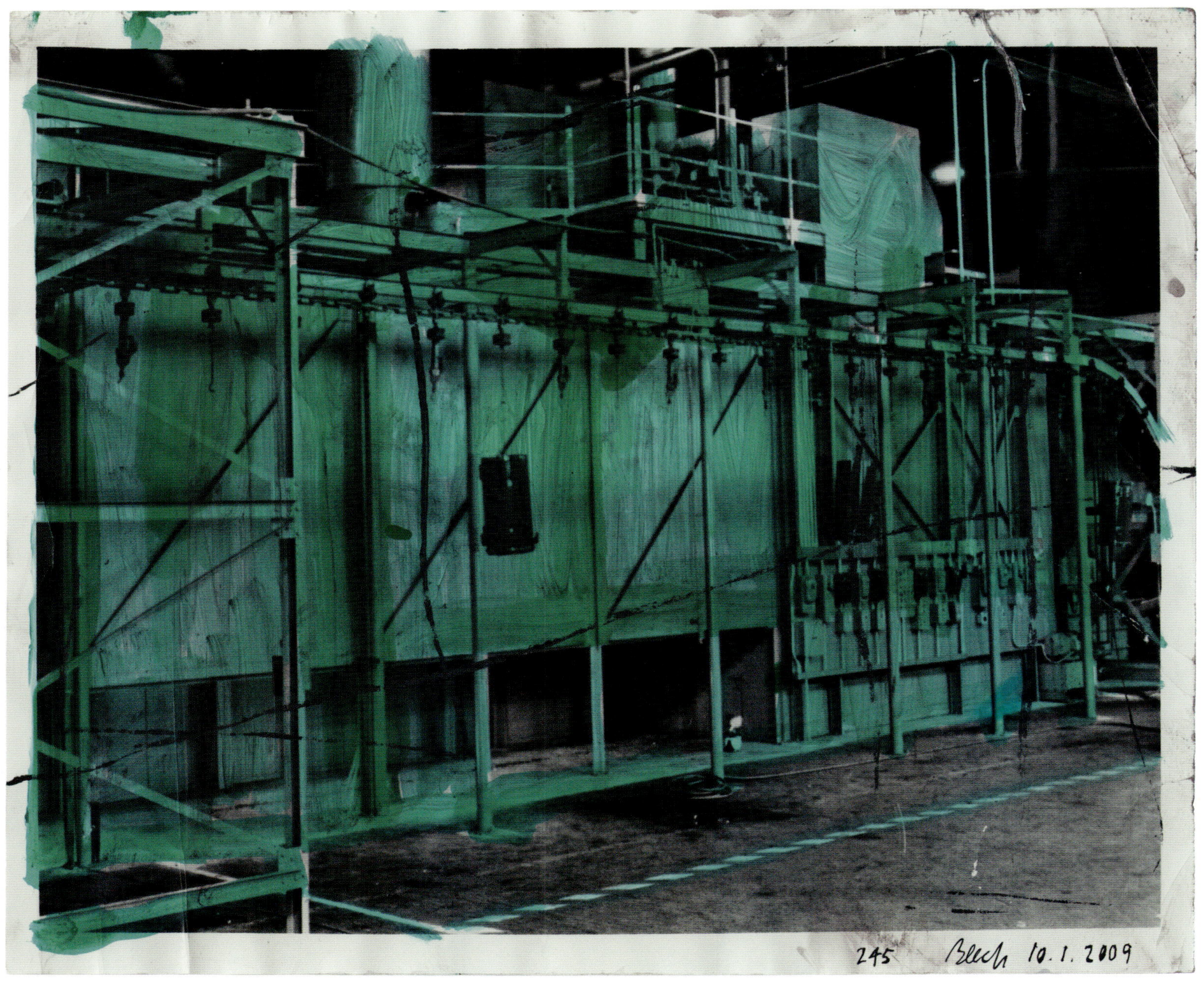
245   Blech 10. 1. 2009

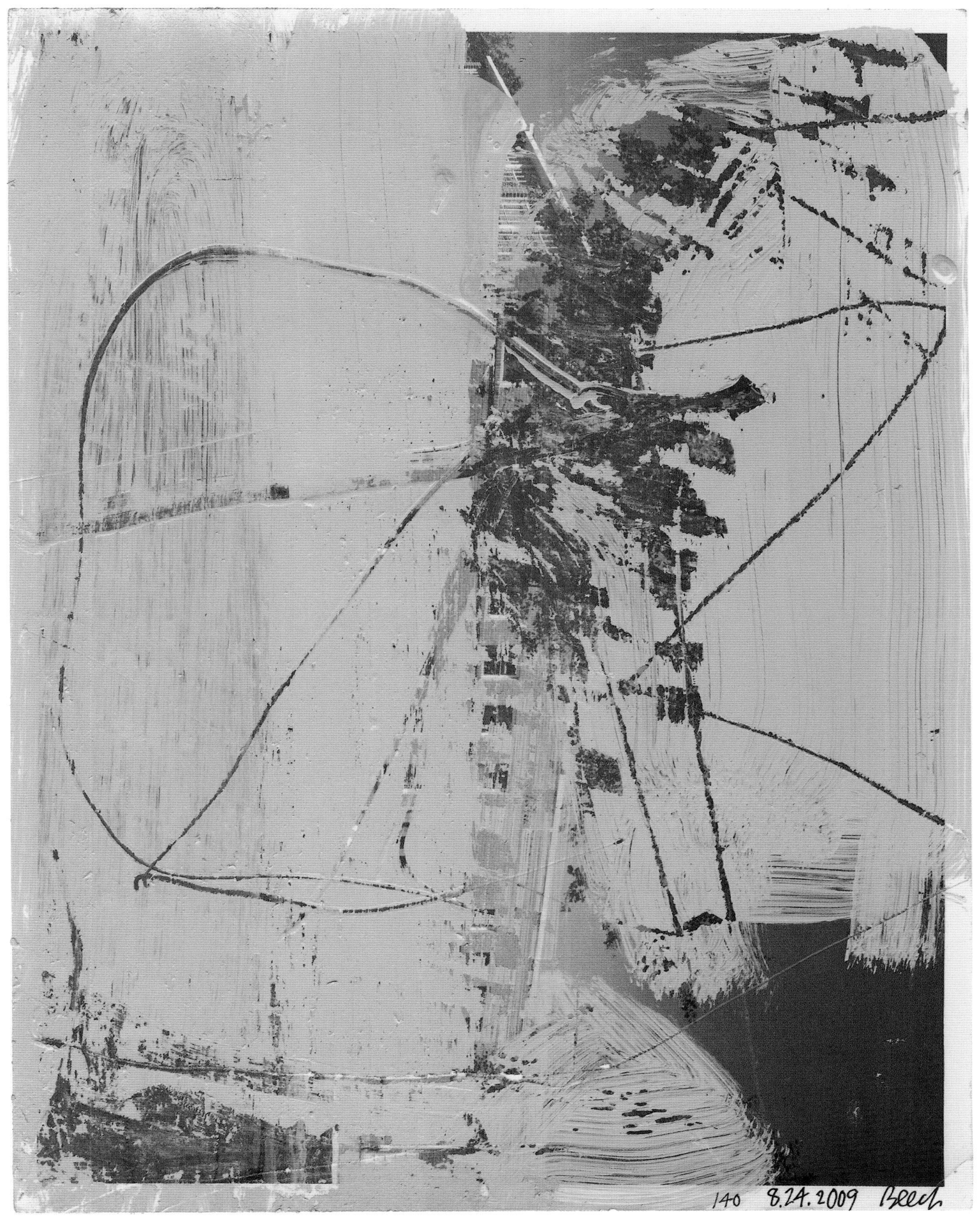
140   8.24.2009   Beech

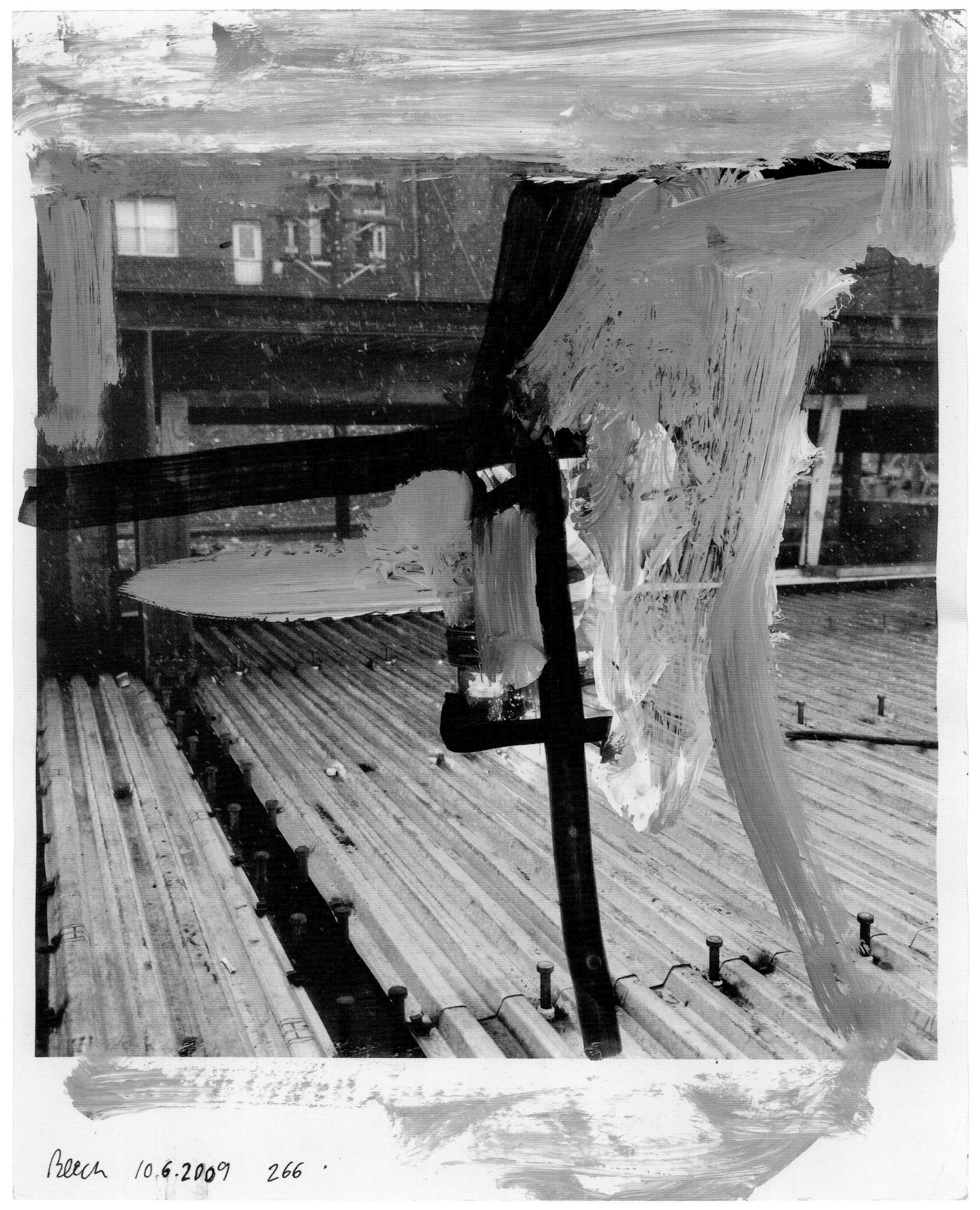

Beech 10.6.2009 266

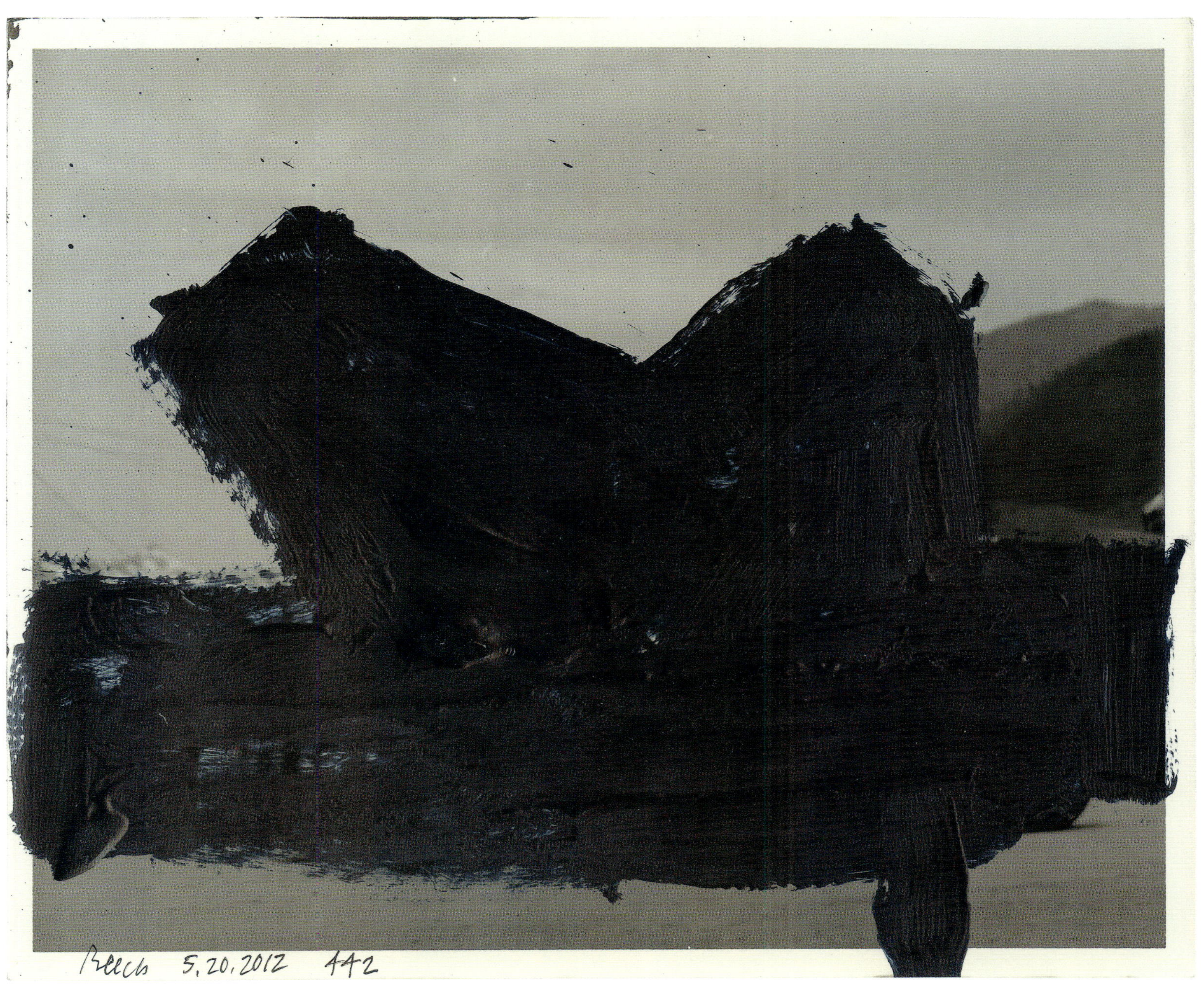
Beech 5.20.2012 442

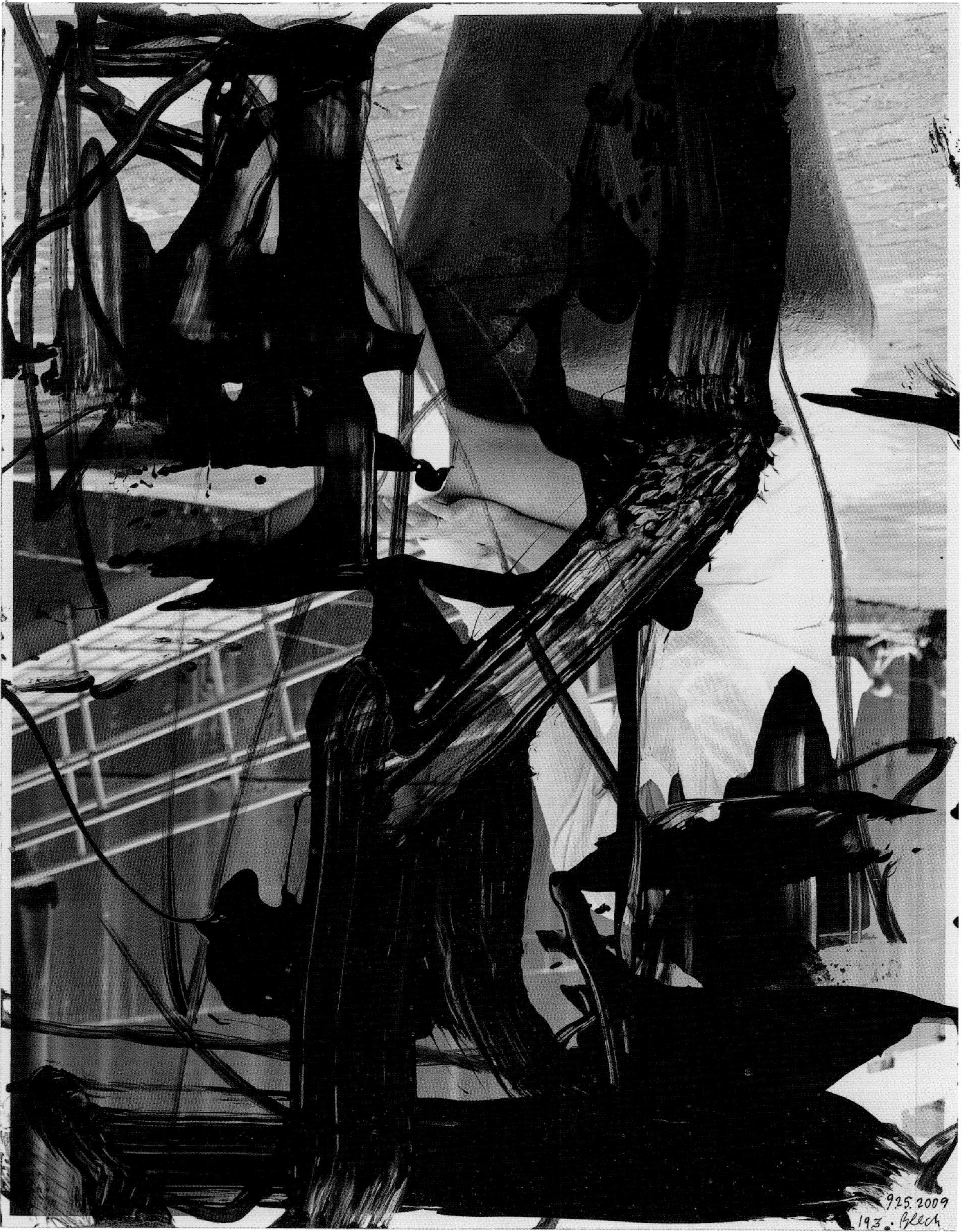

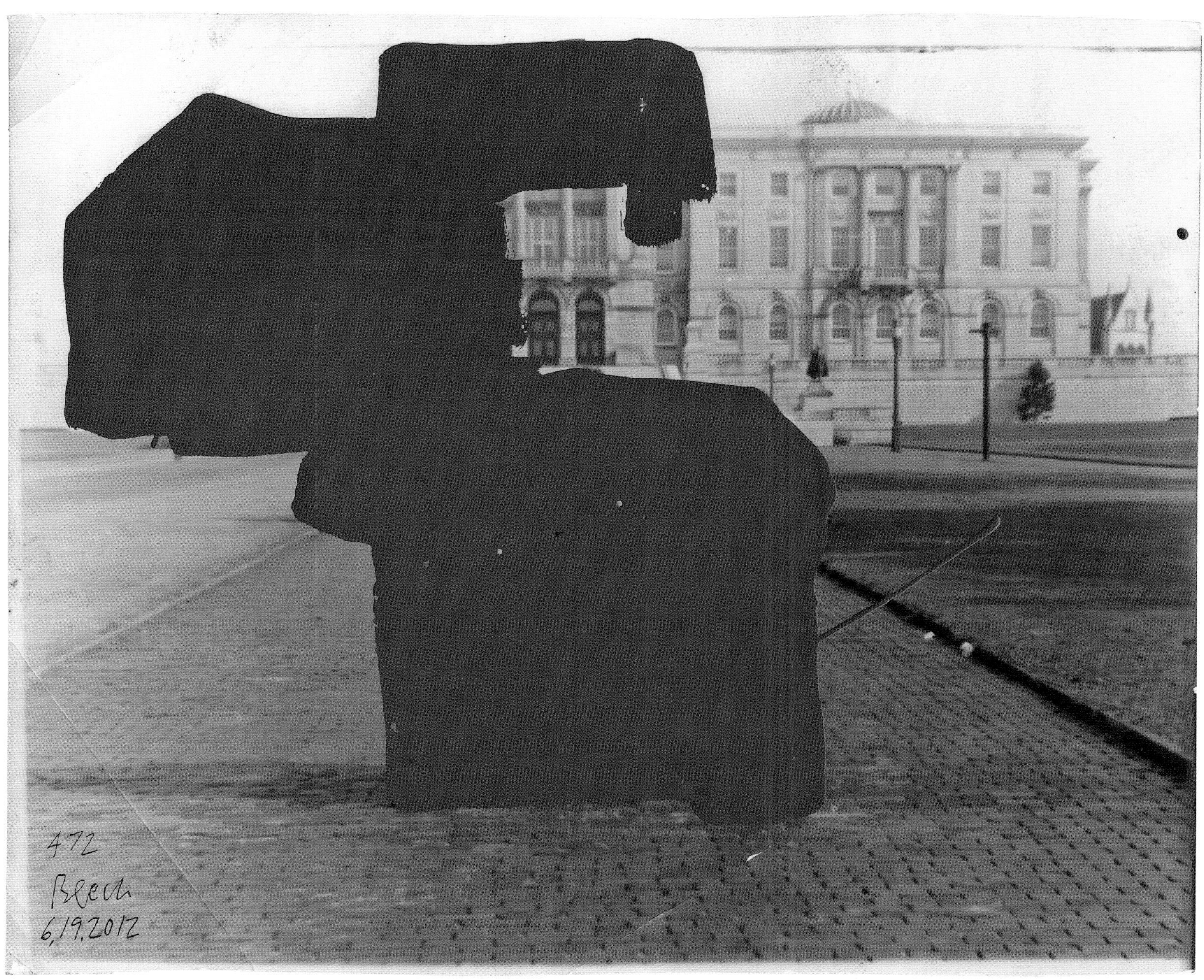
472
Beech
6.19.2012

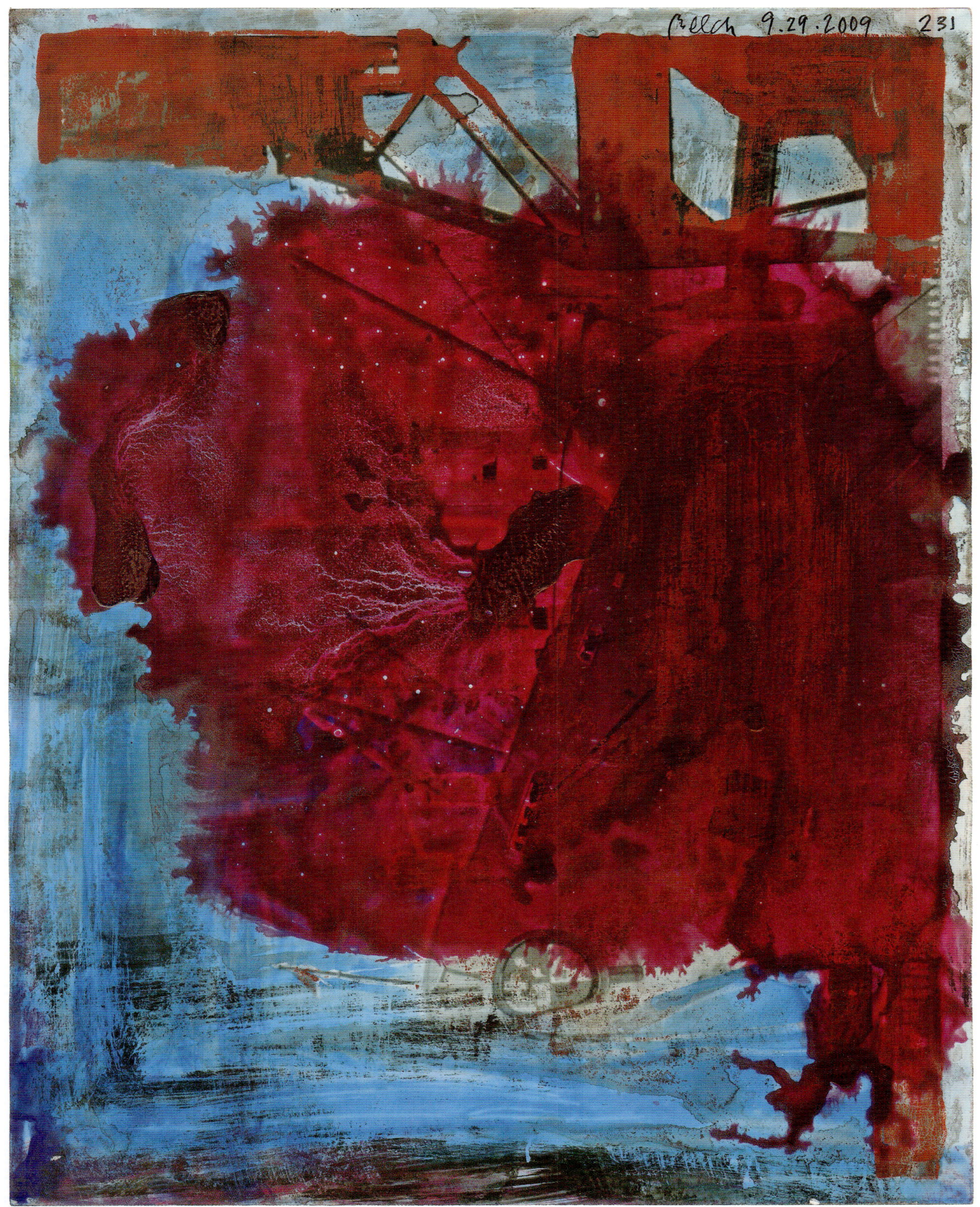
Welch 9.29.2009   231

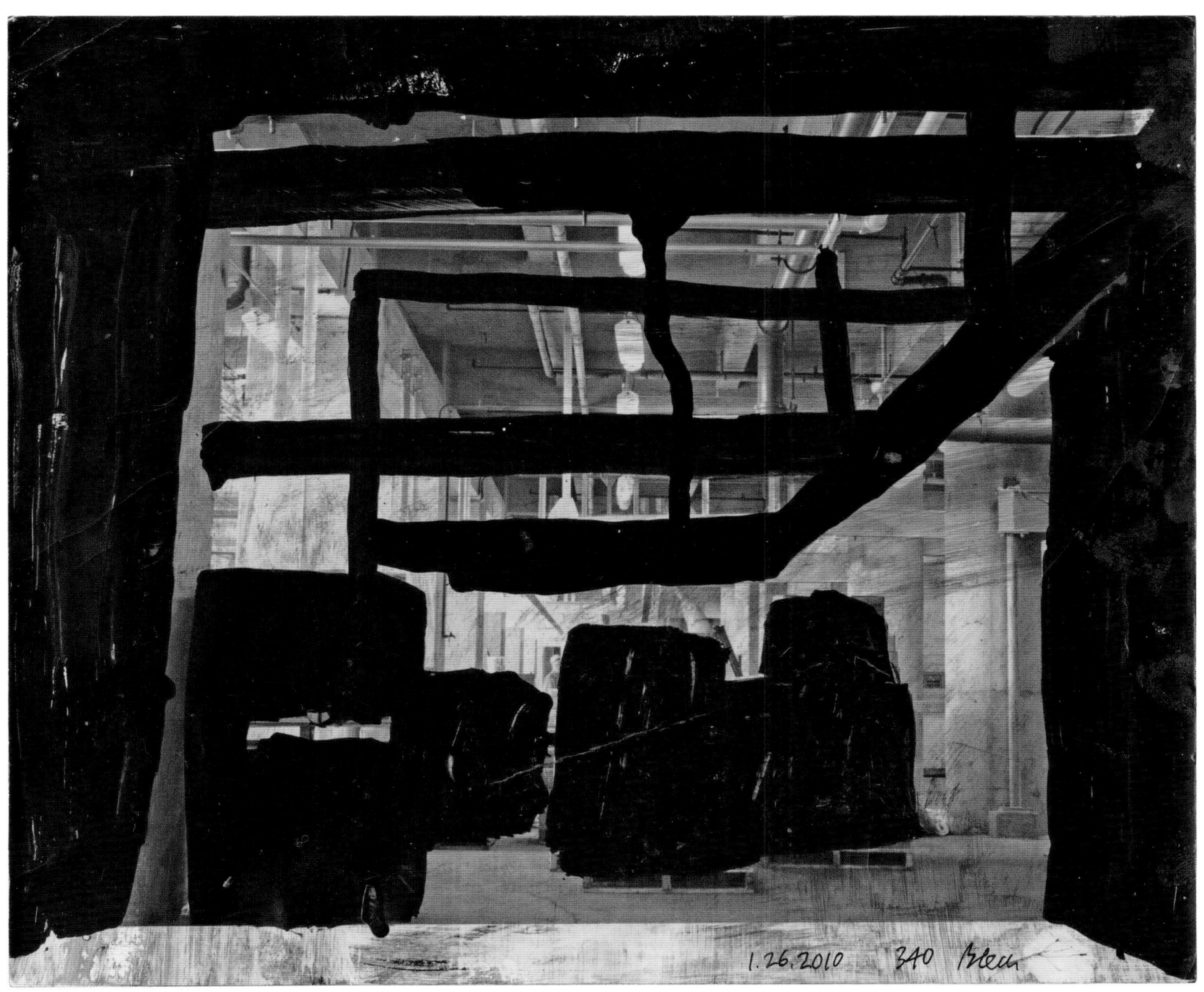

1.26.2010   340   Bloch

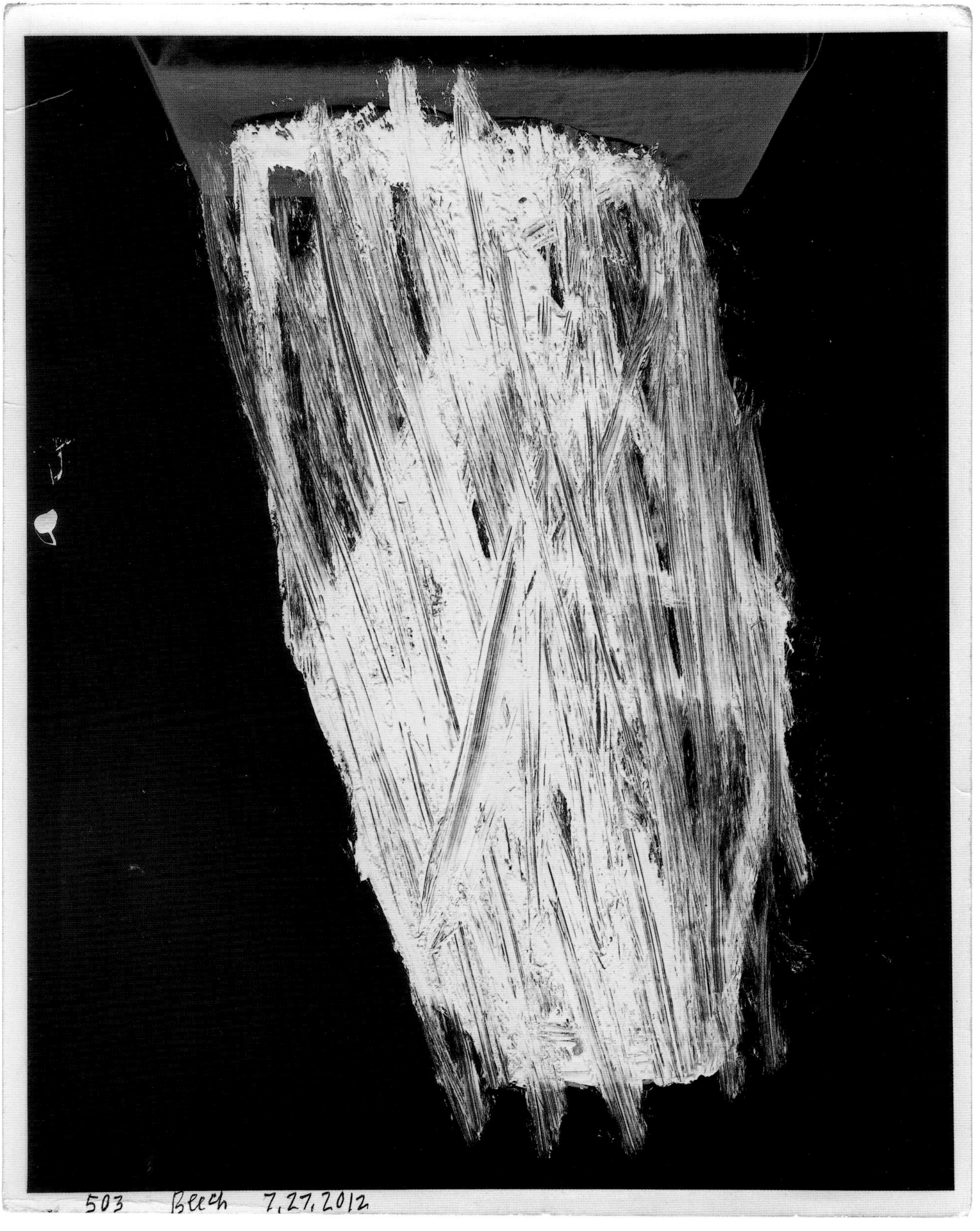

503   Beech   7.27.2012

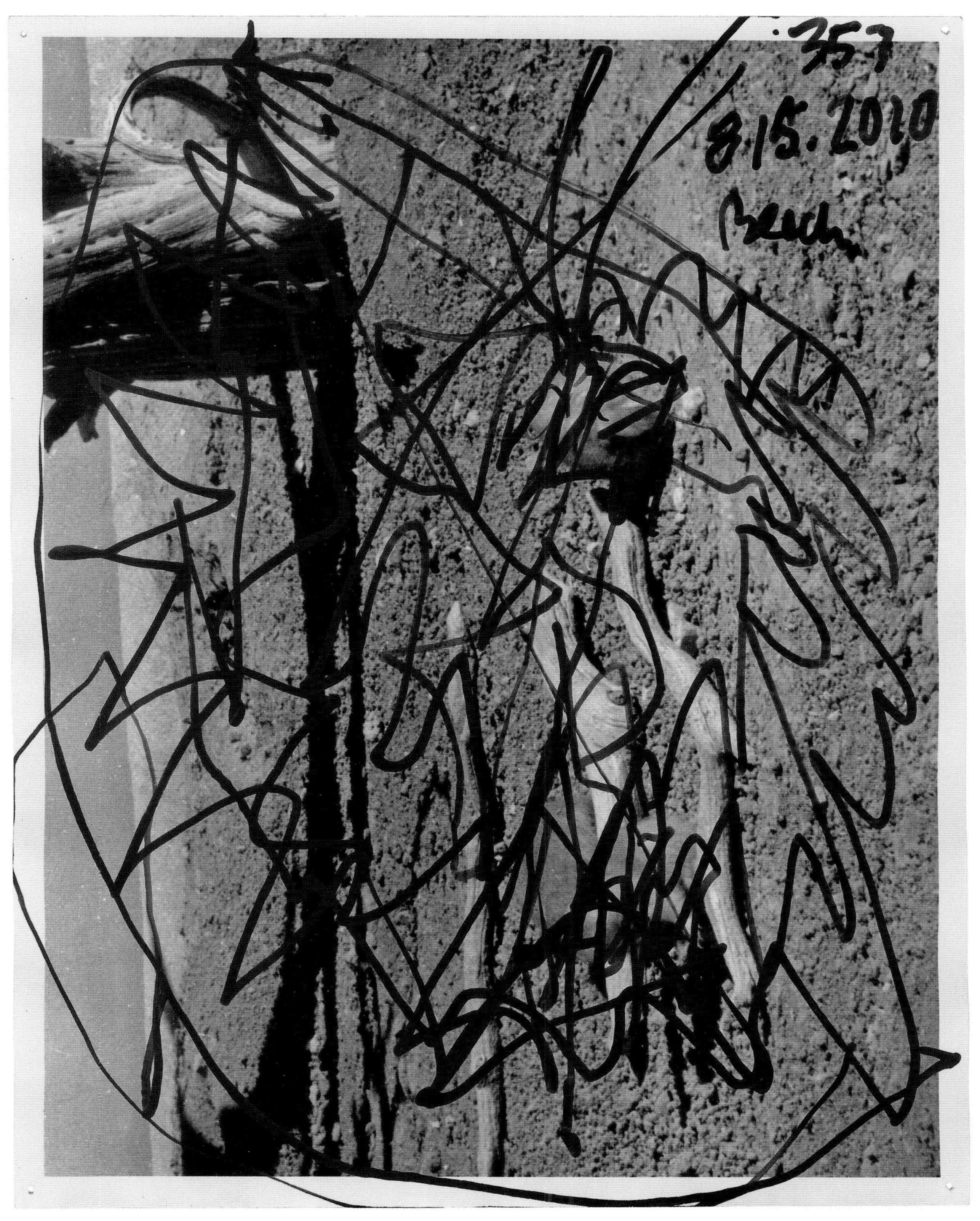
357
8.15.2020

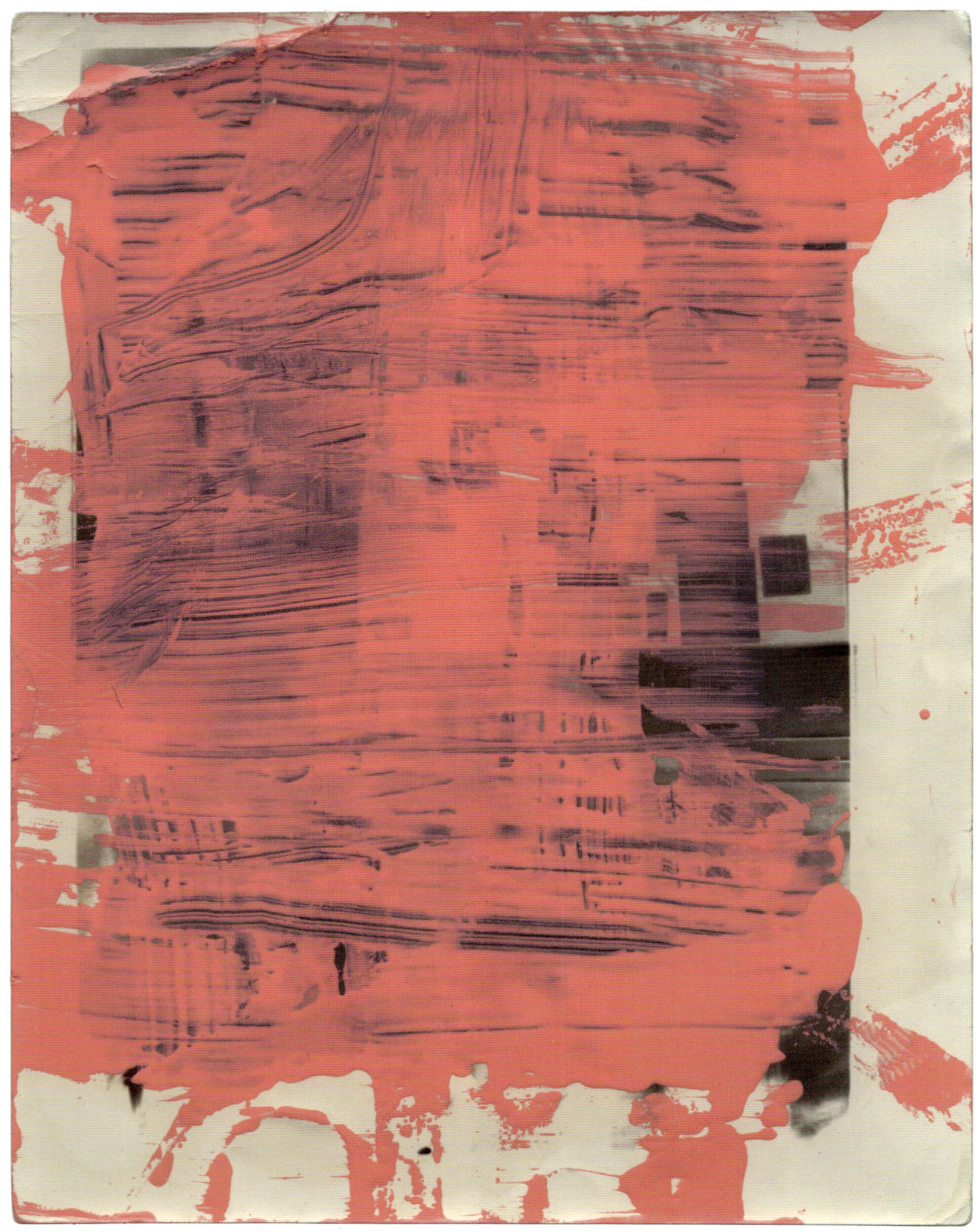

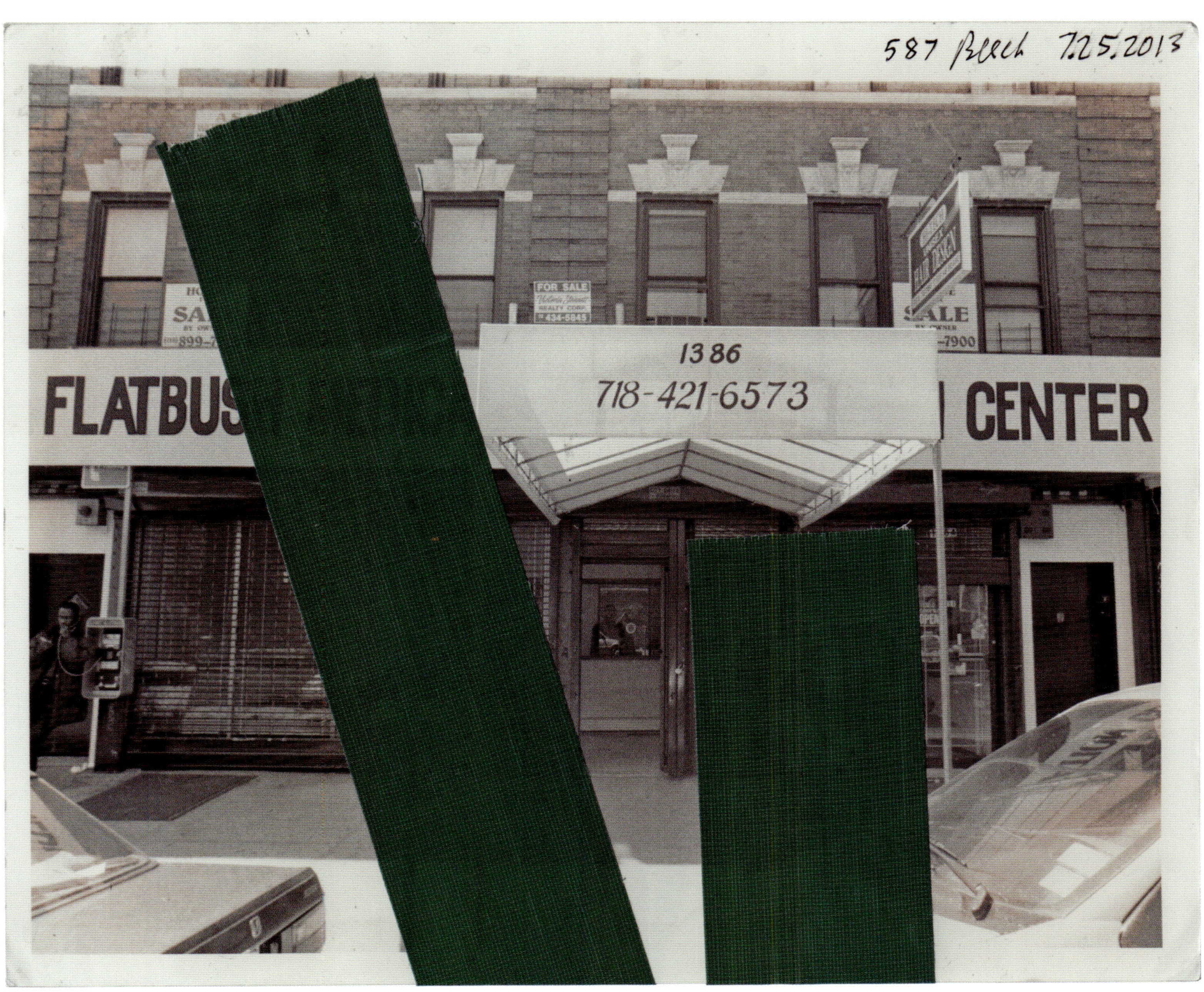
587 Beech 7.25.2013
FLATBUS
CENTER
1386
718-421-6573
FOR SALE
Nelson Street
REALTY CORP.
434-5845
SALE
BY OWNER
7900

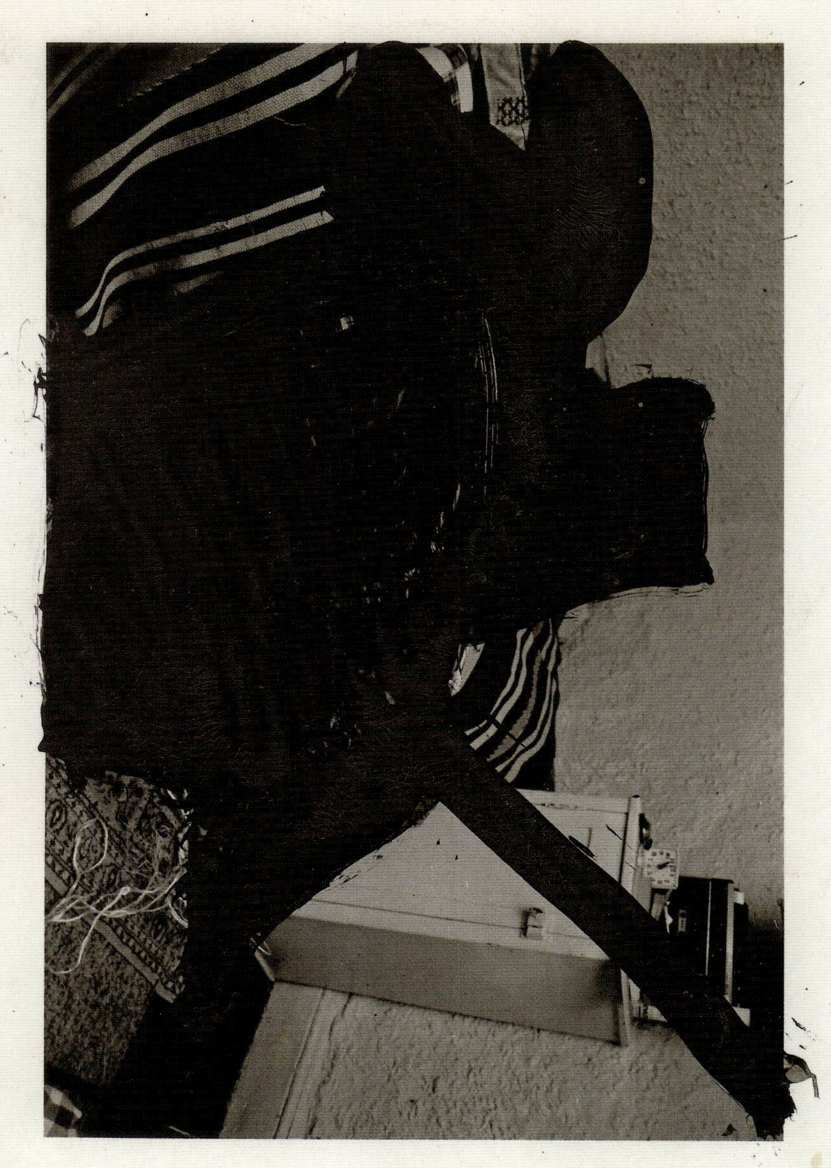

435 Bleich 4.25.2012

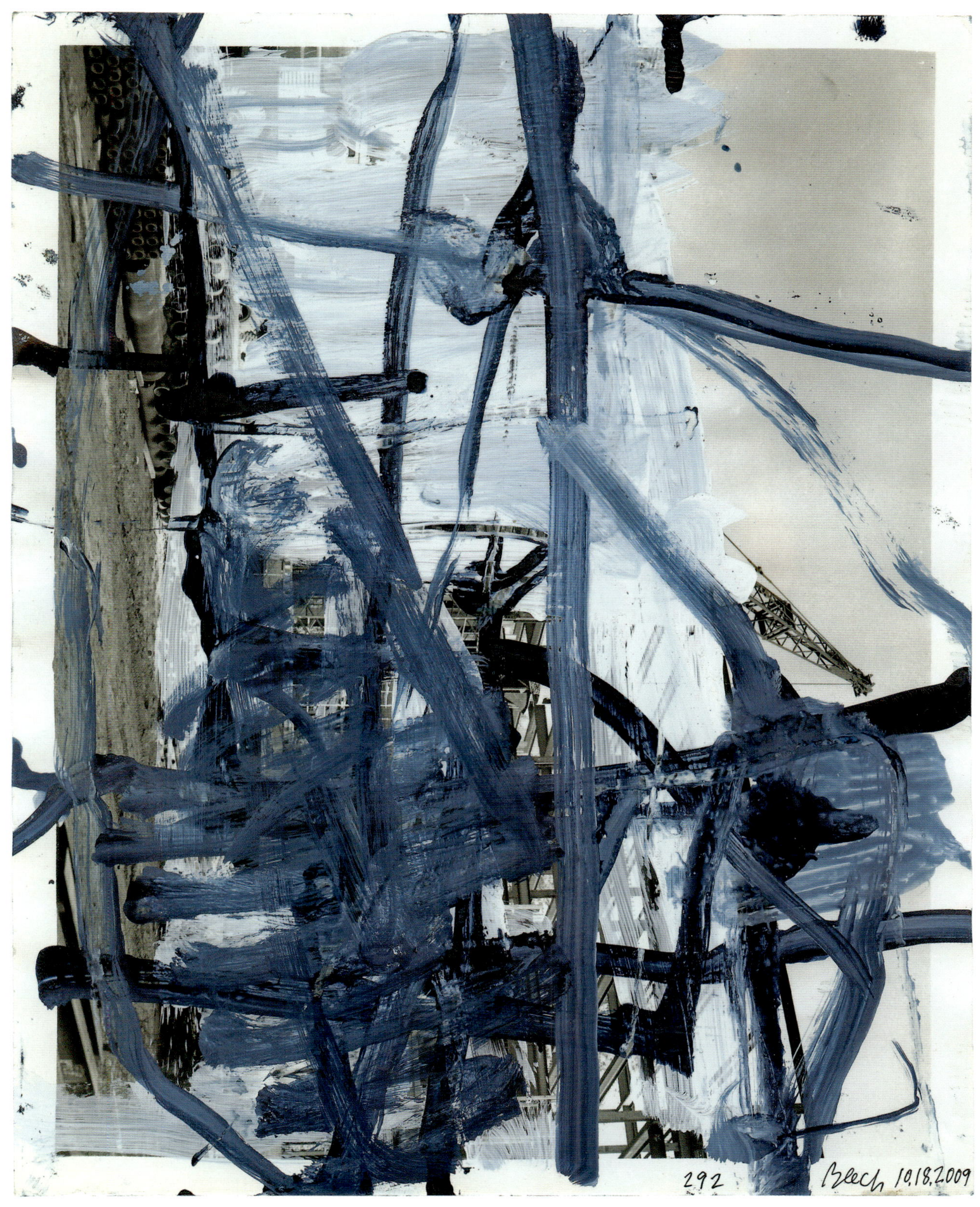

292
Blech 10.18.2009

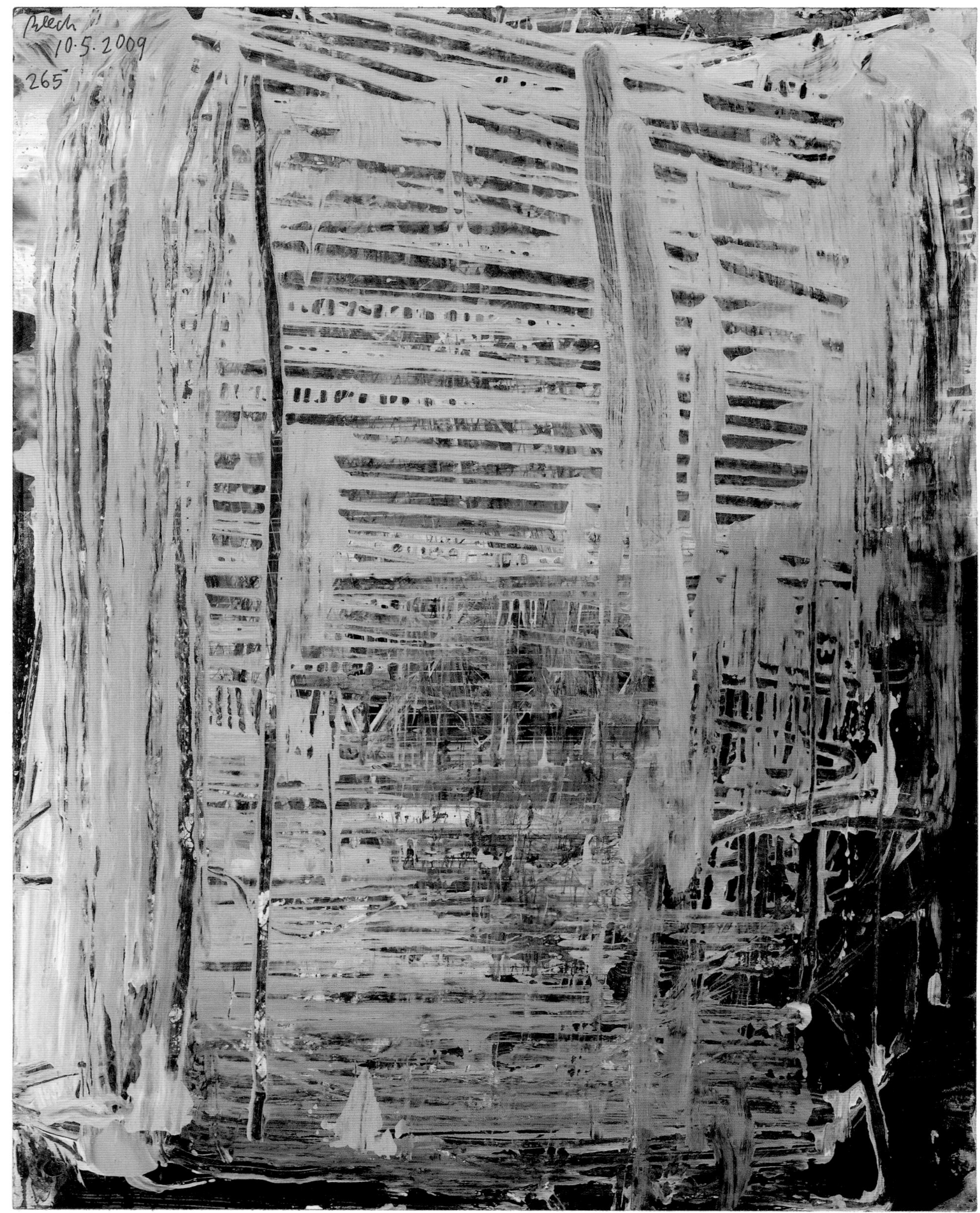Blech
10·5·2009
265

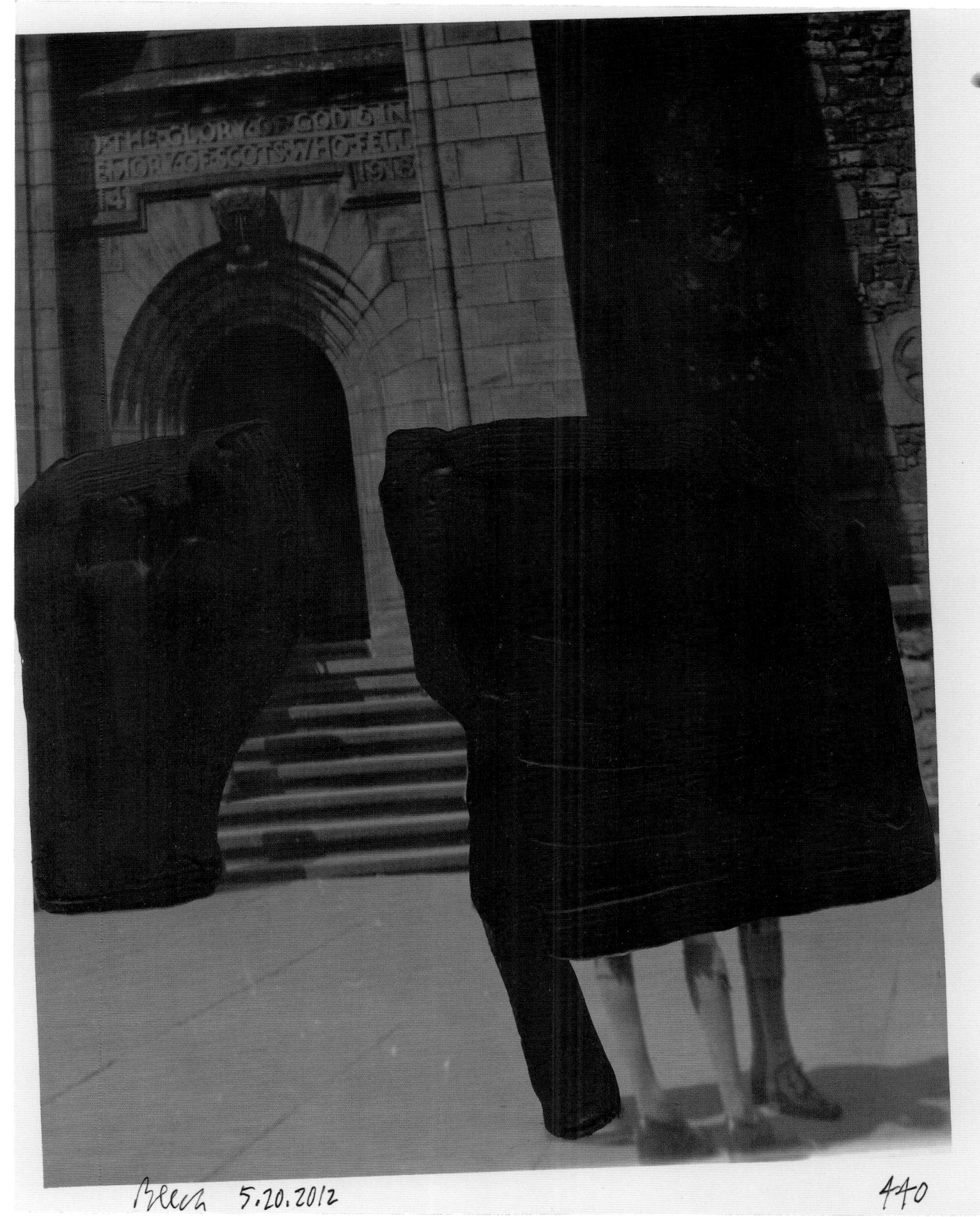

Beech 5.20.2012

440

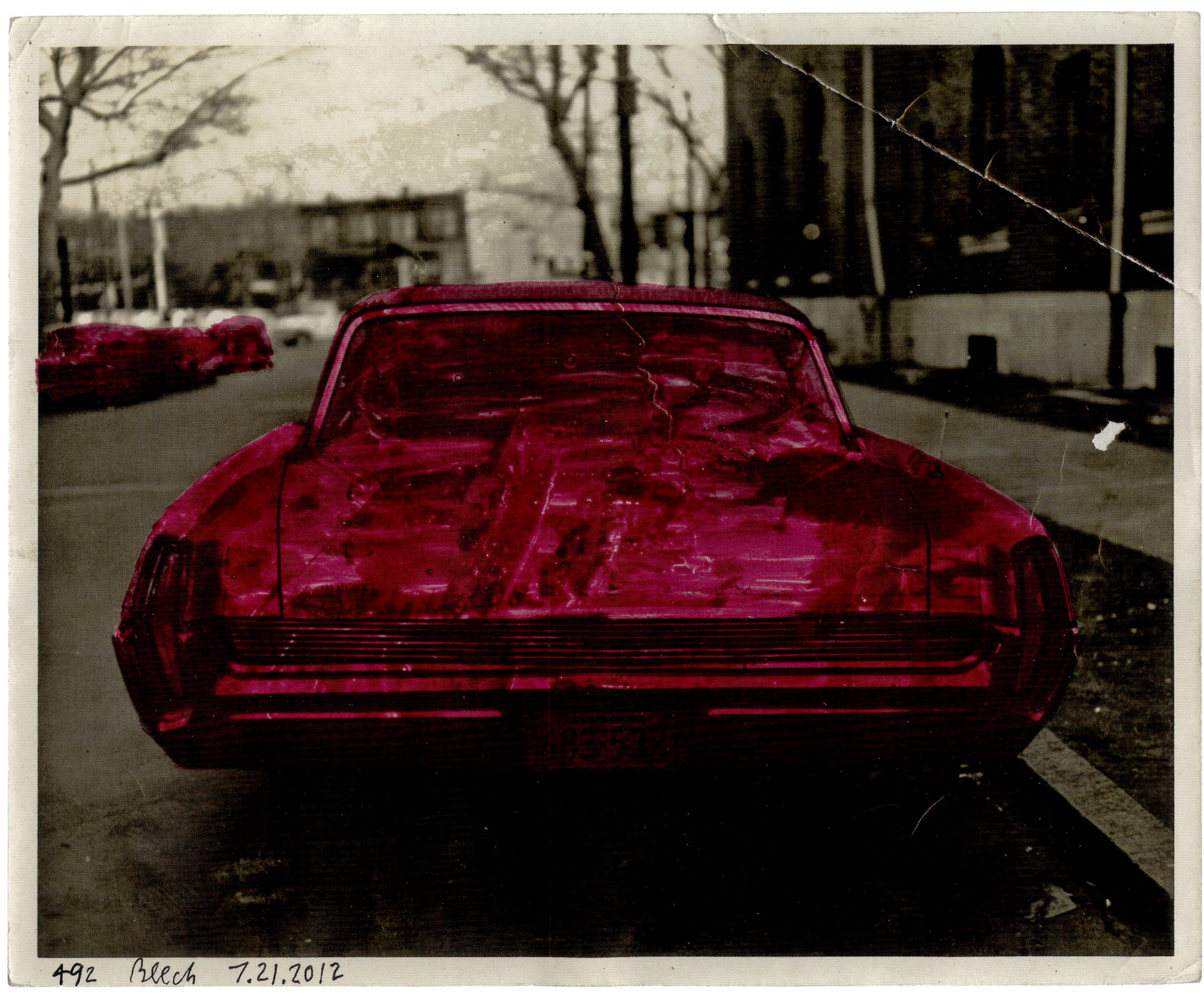

492   Blech   7.21.2012

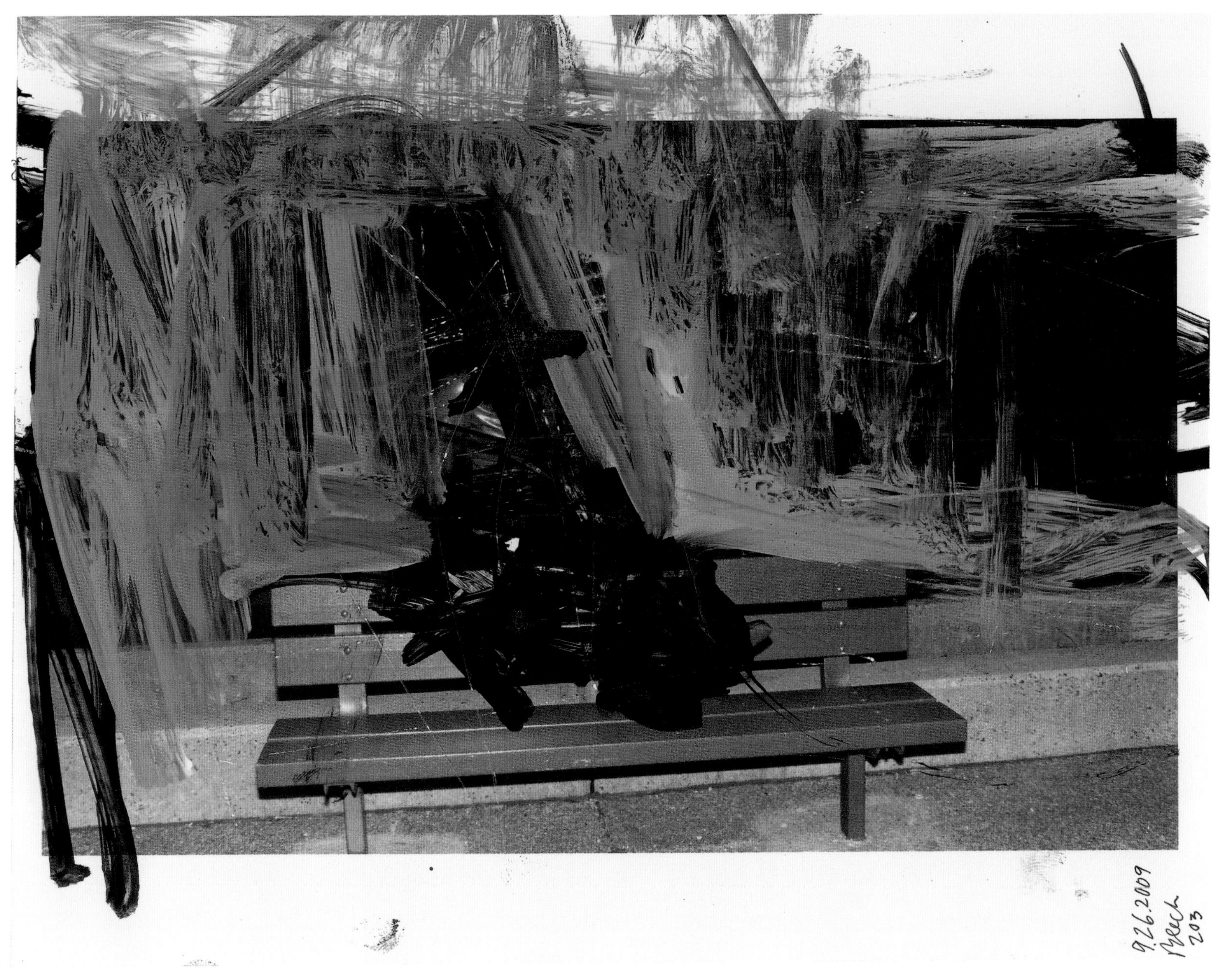

9.26.2009
Beech
203

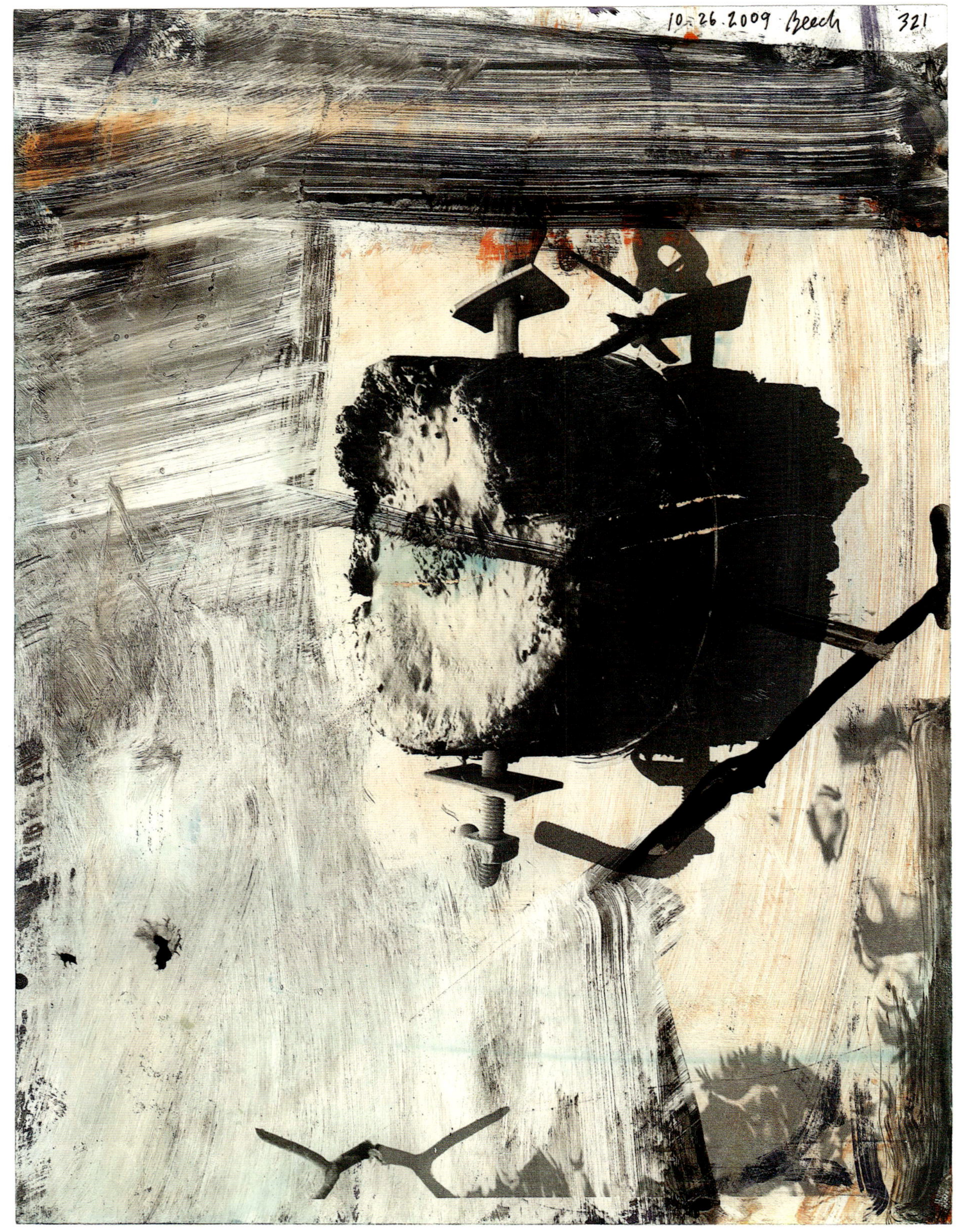

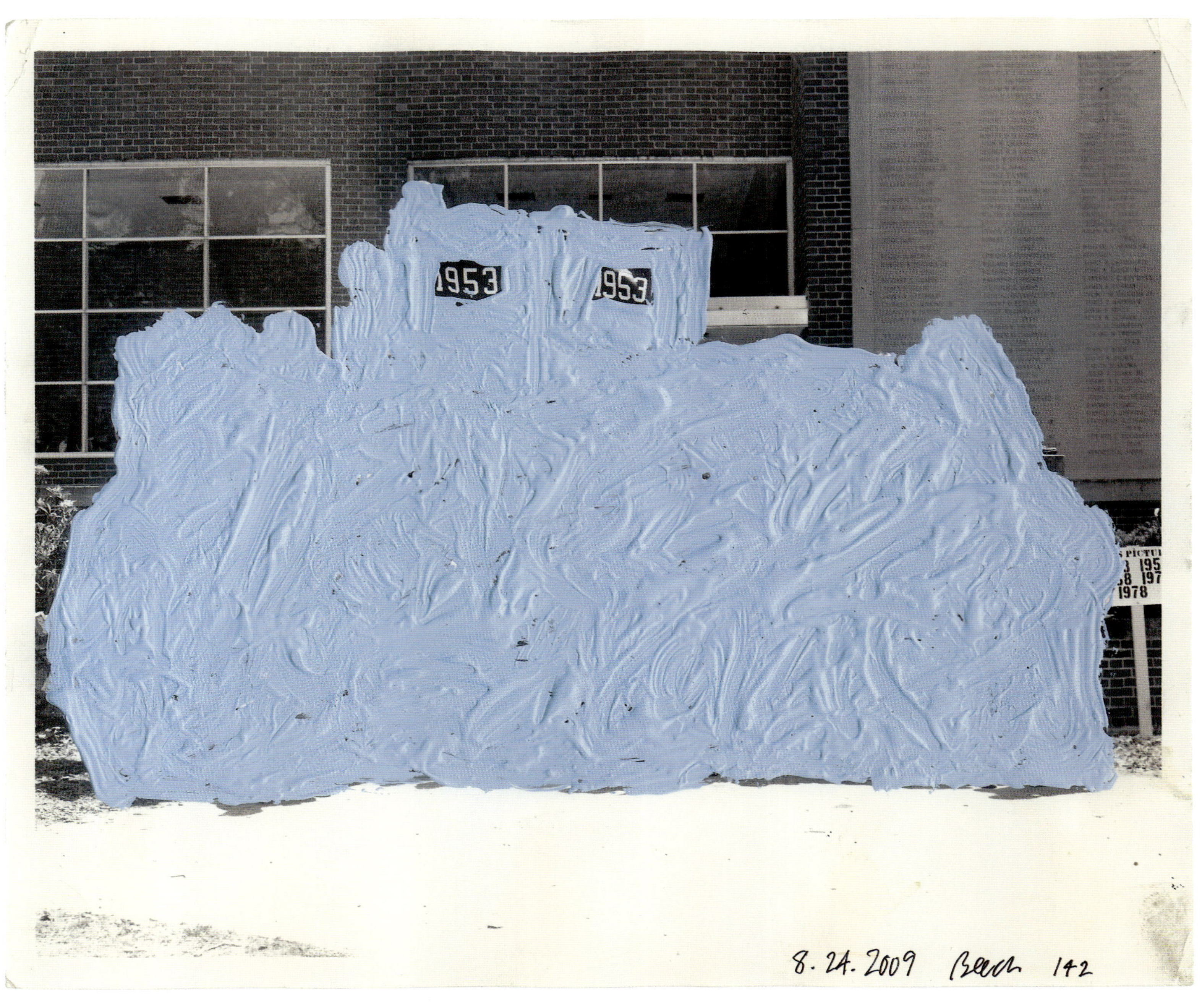

35

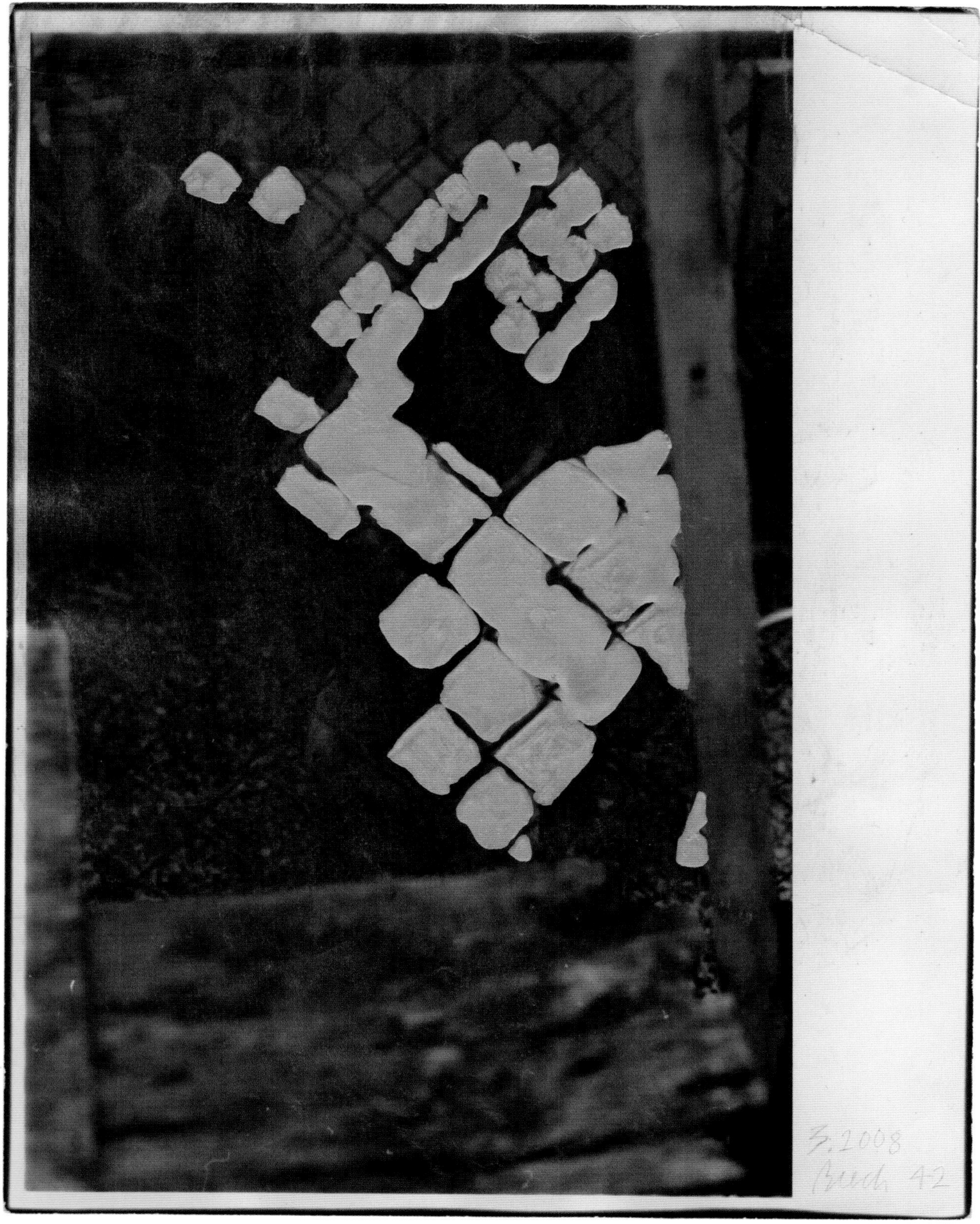

3.2008
Buch 42

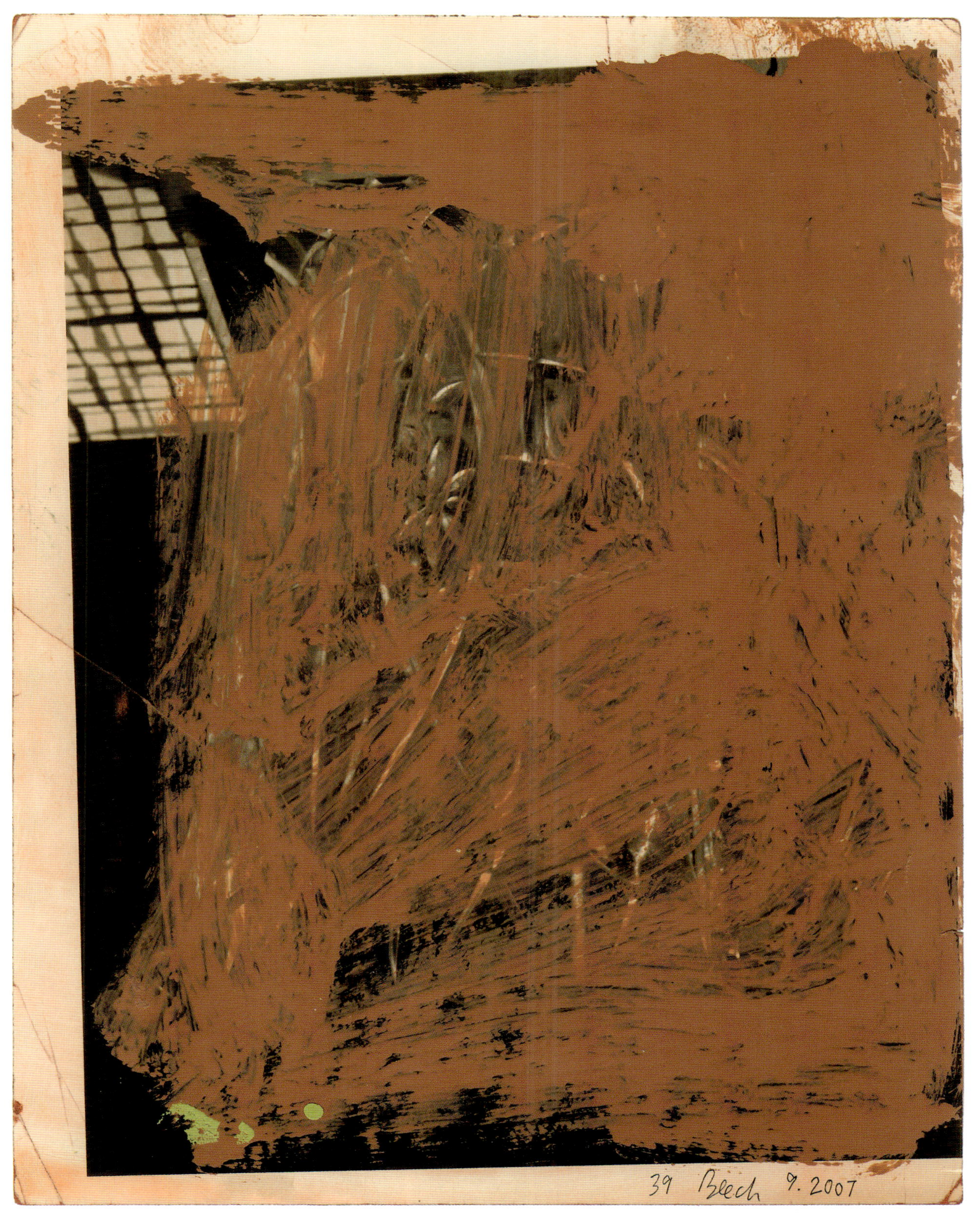
39 Blech 9. 2007

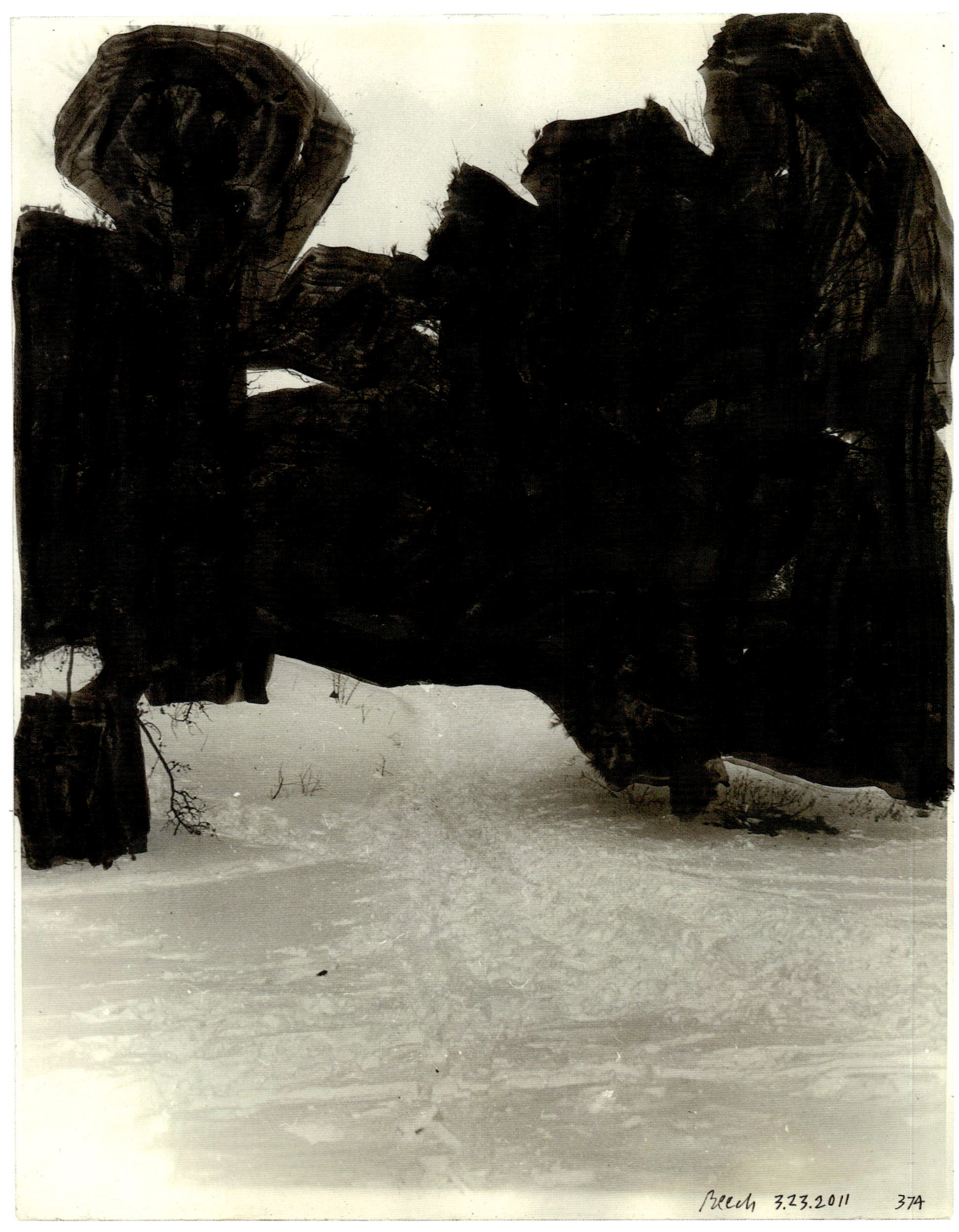

Beech 3.23.2011   374

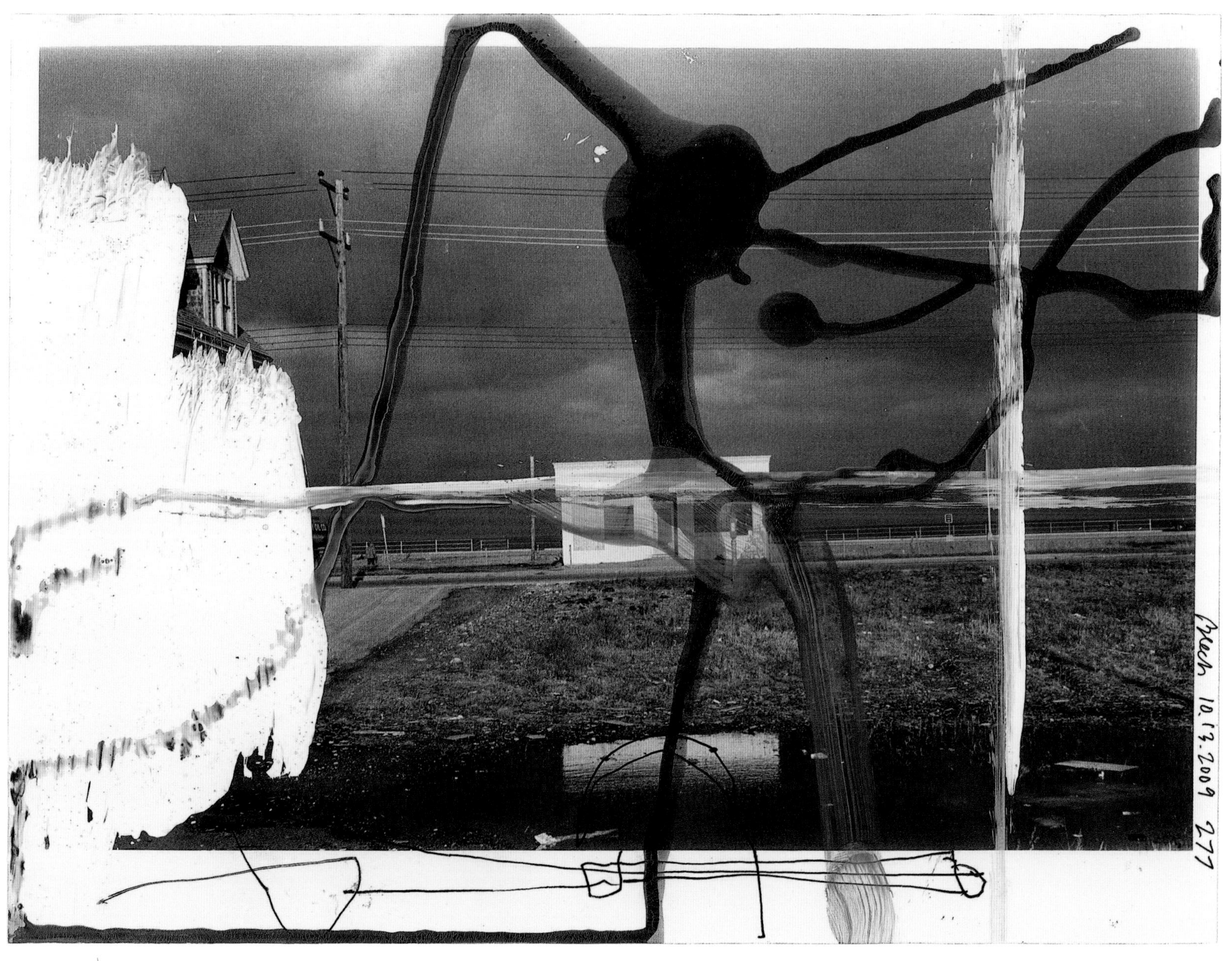

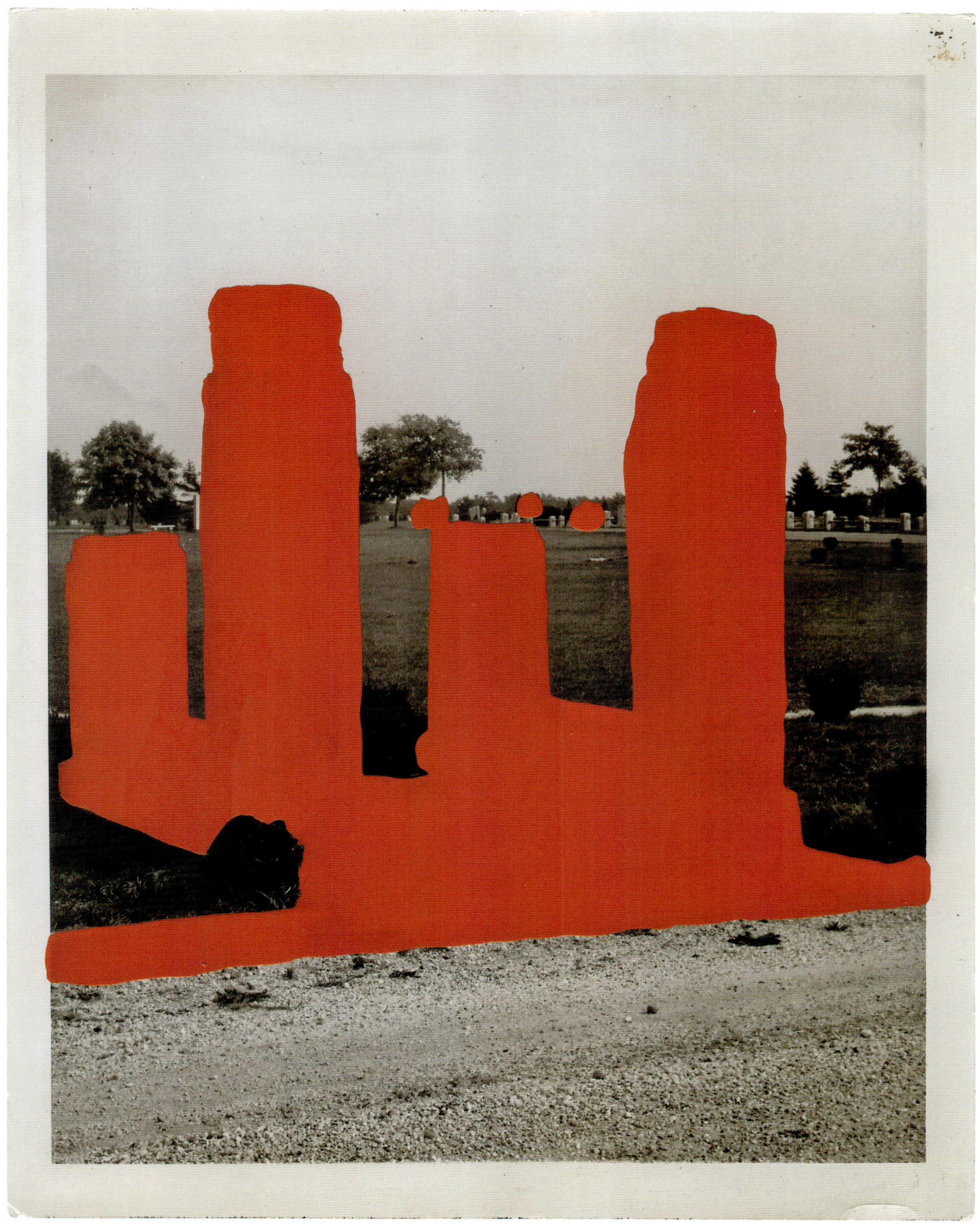

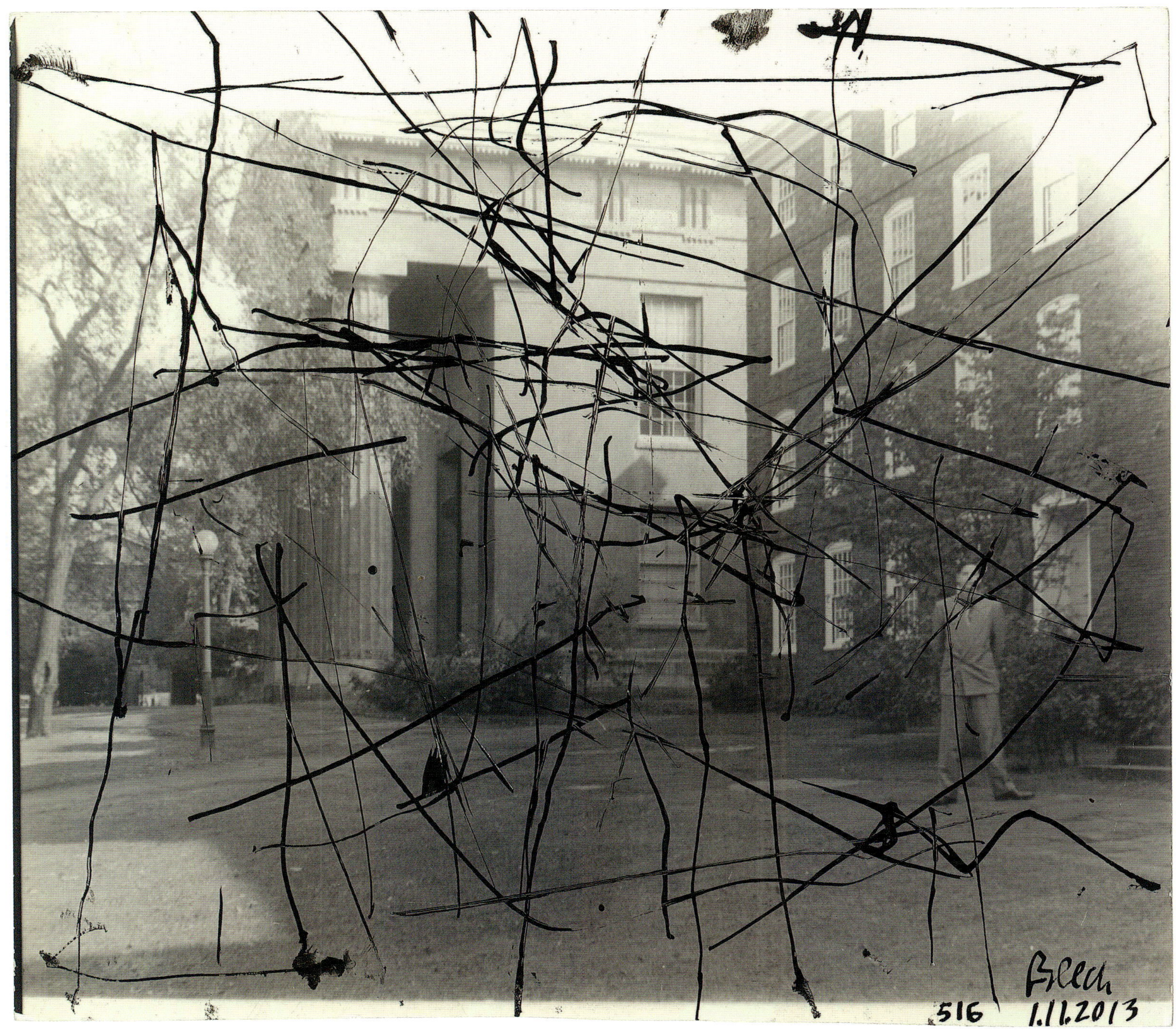

Beech
516   1.11.2013

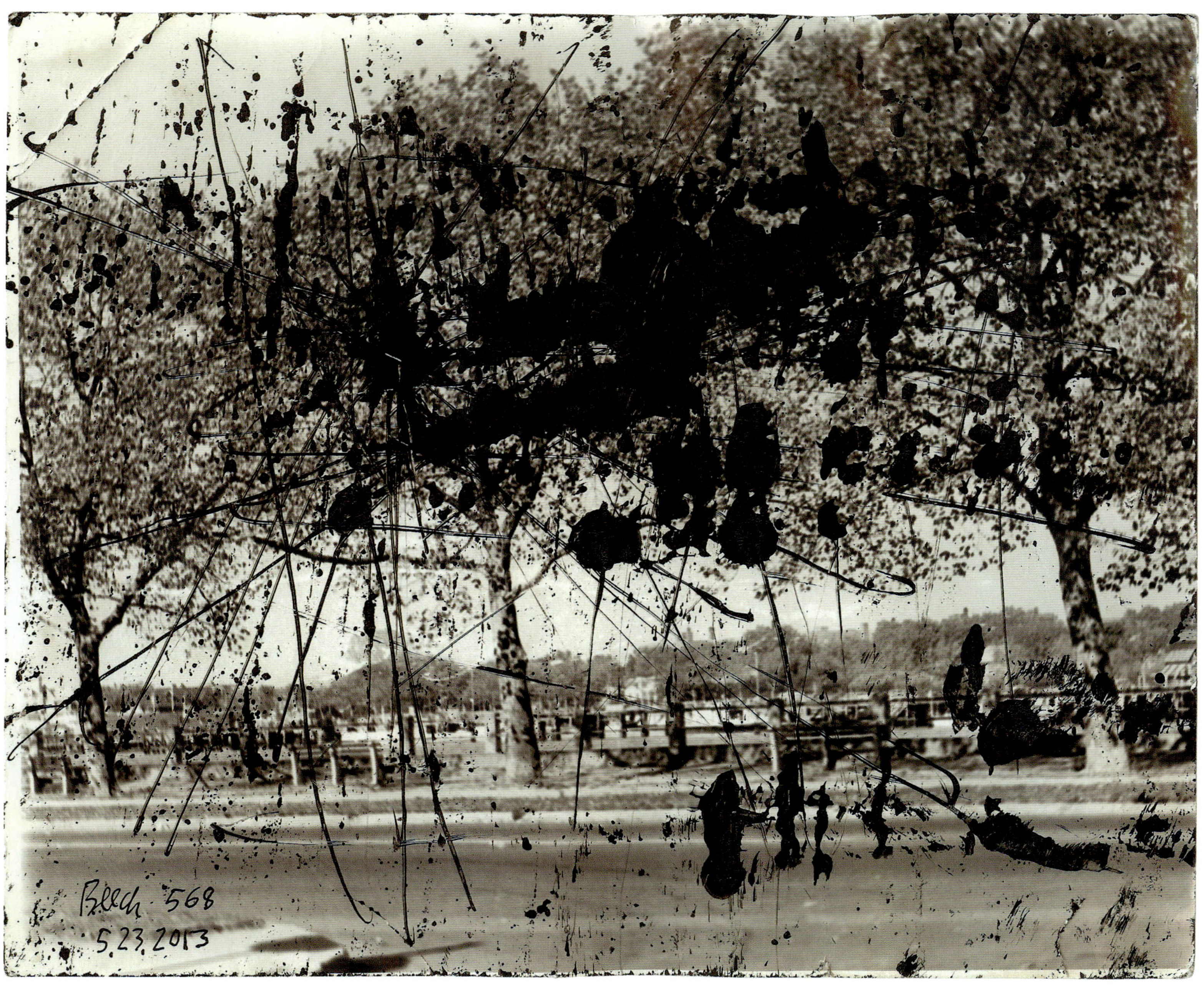
Beech 568
5.23.2013

8.27.2009 Beech 151

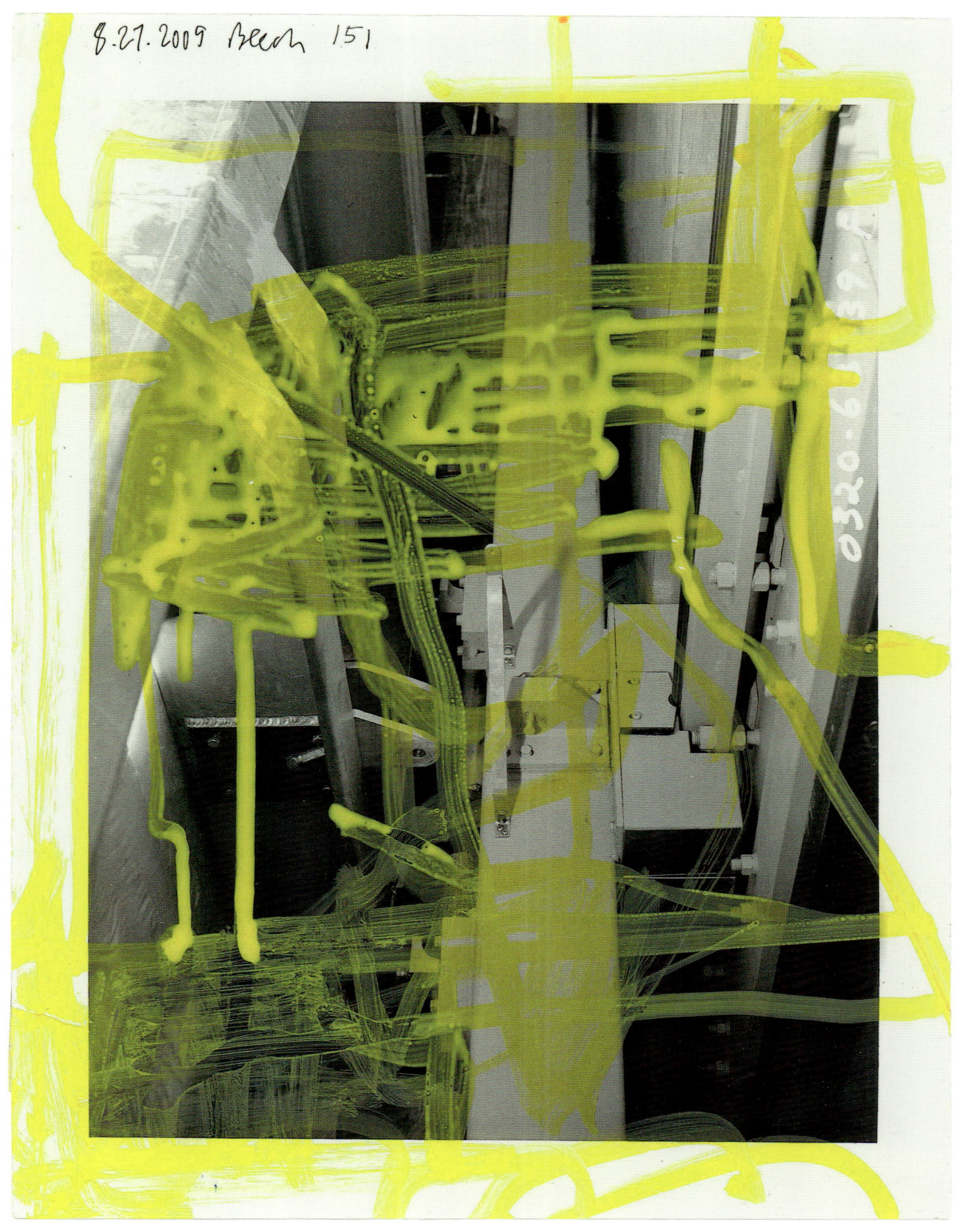

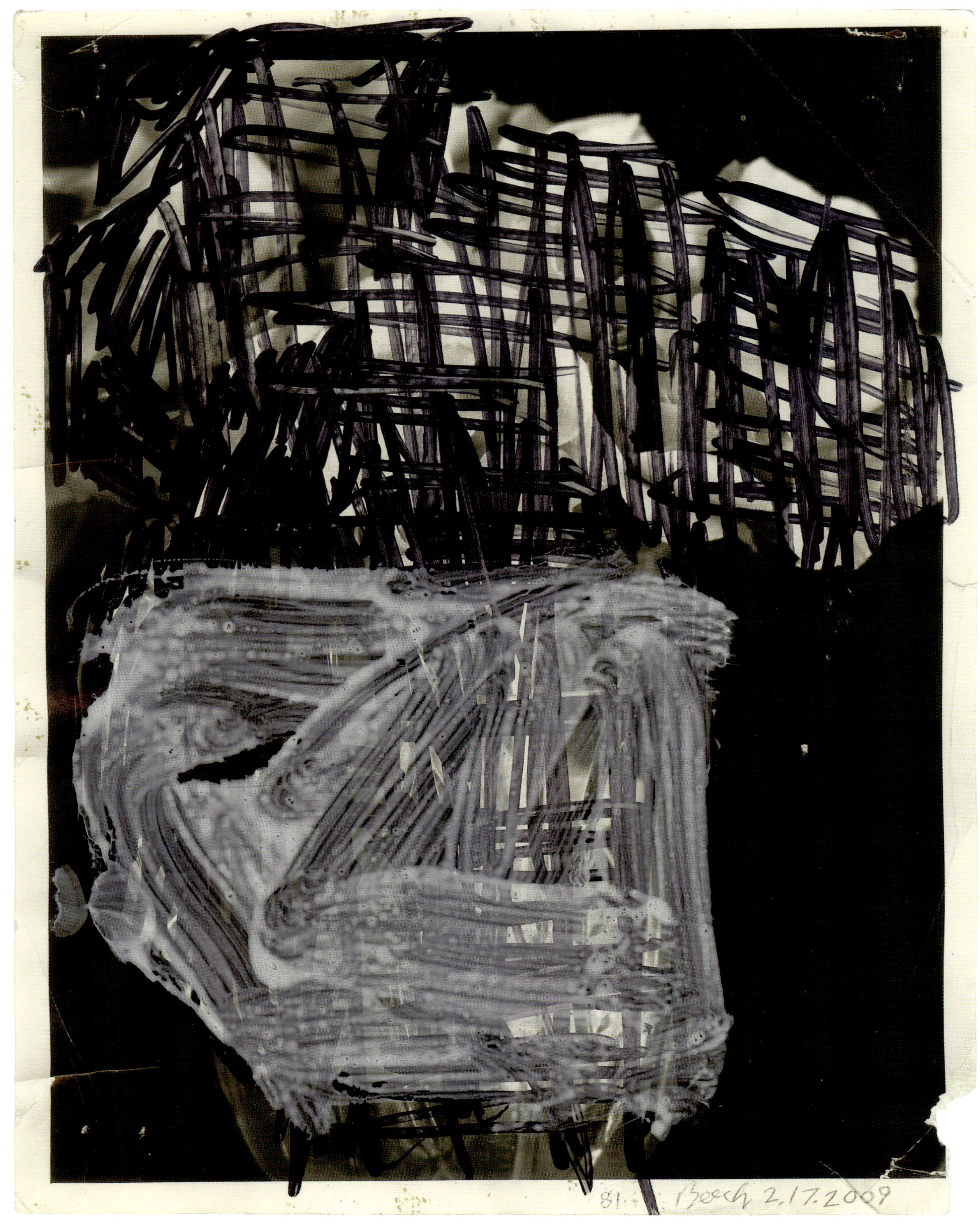
81 Beech 2.17.2009

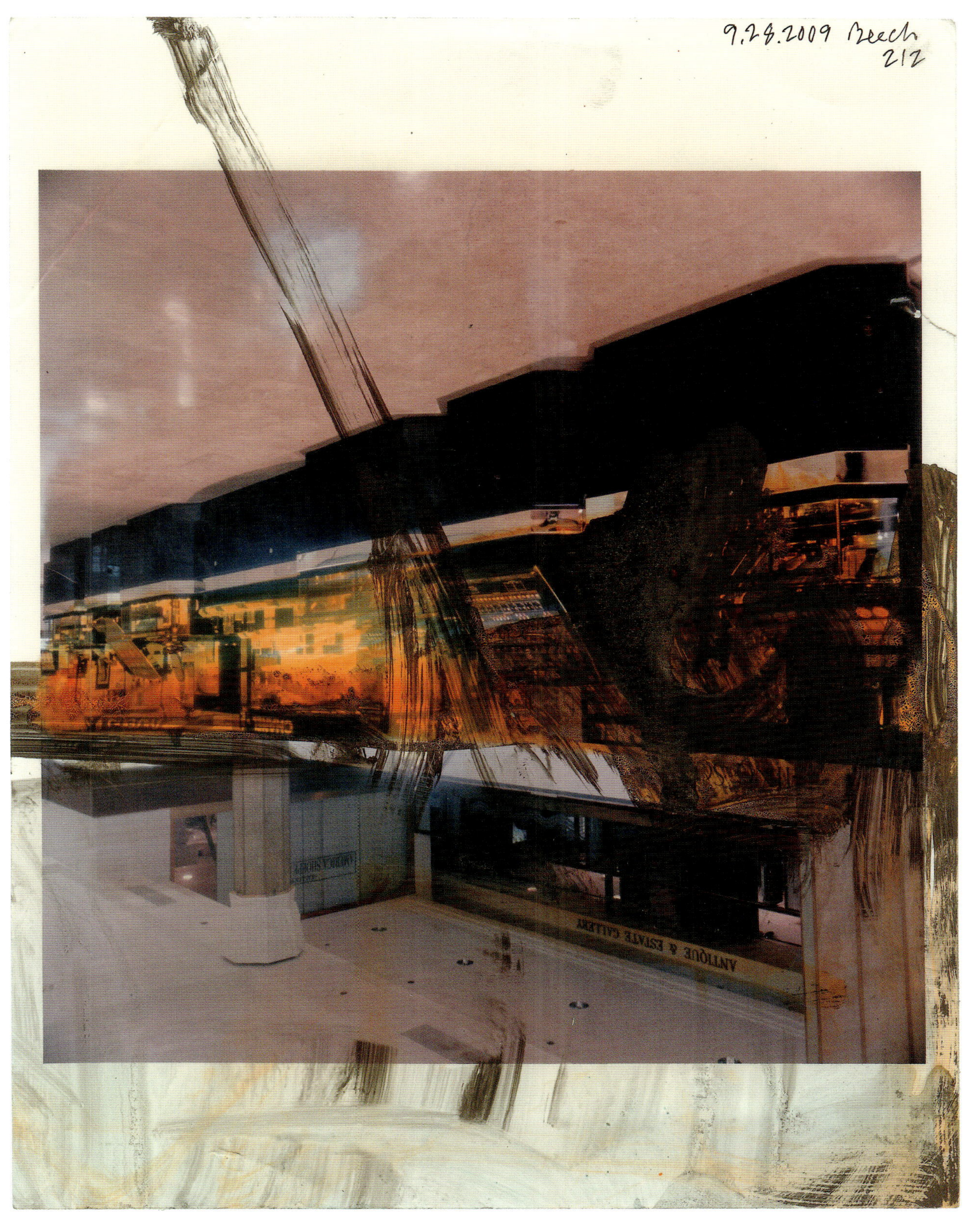
ANTIQUE & ESTATE GALLERY

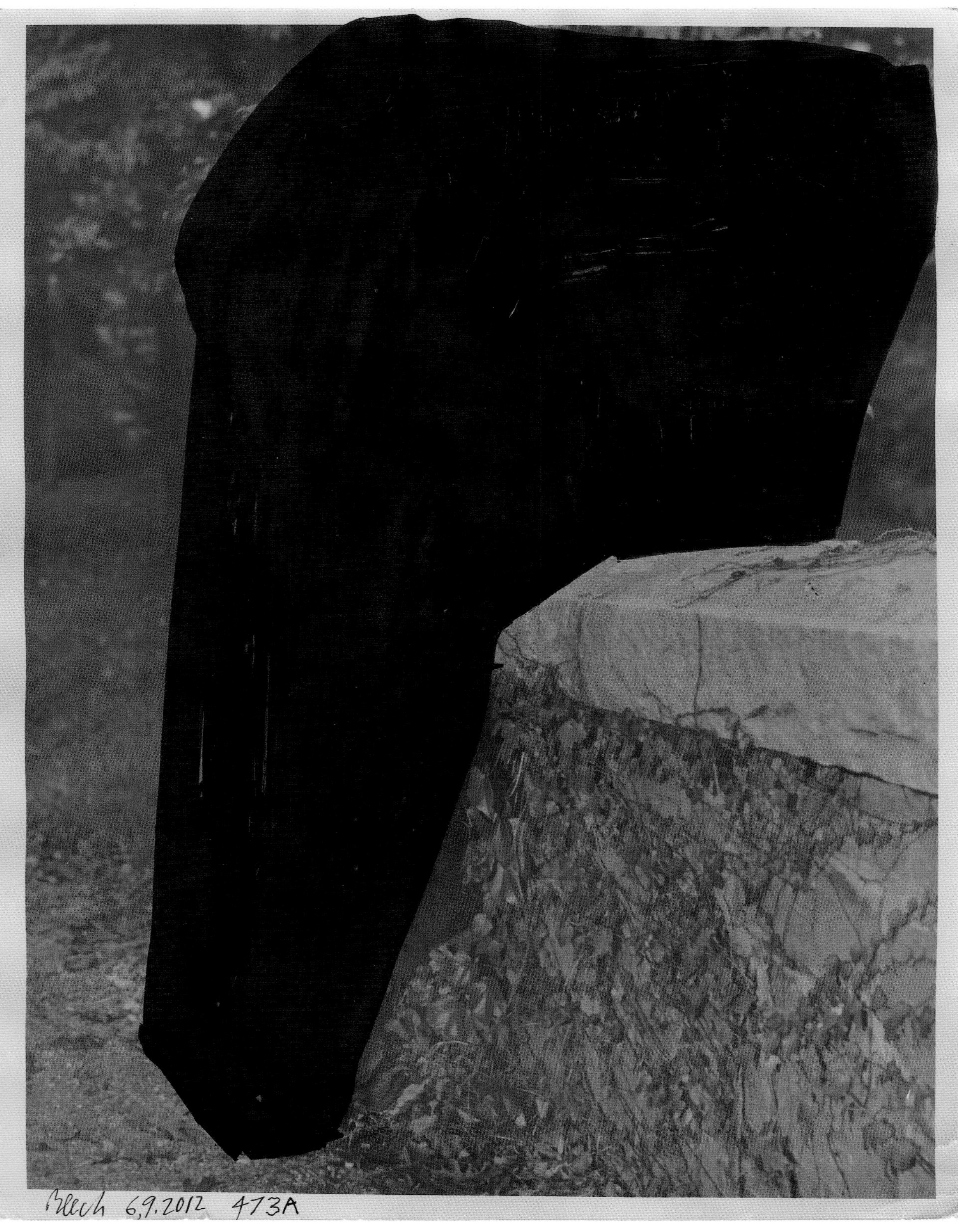
Blech 6.9.2012   473A

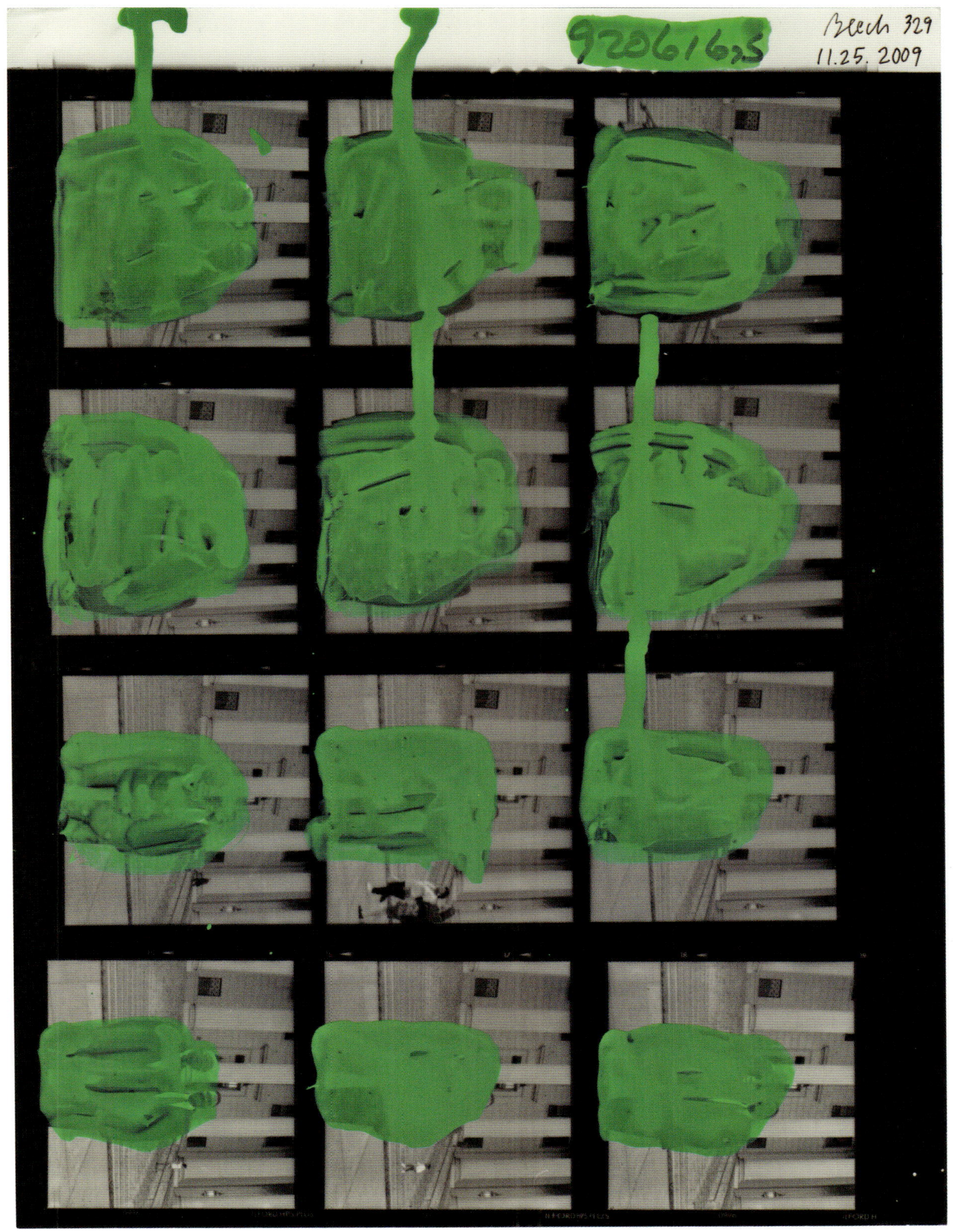

47

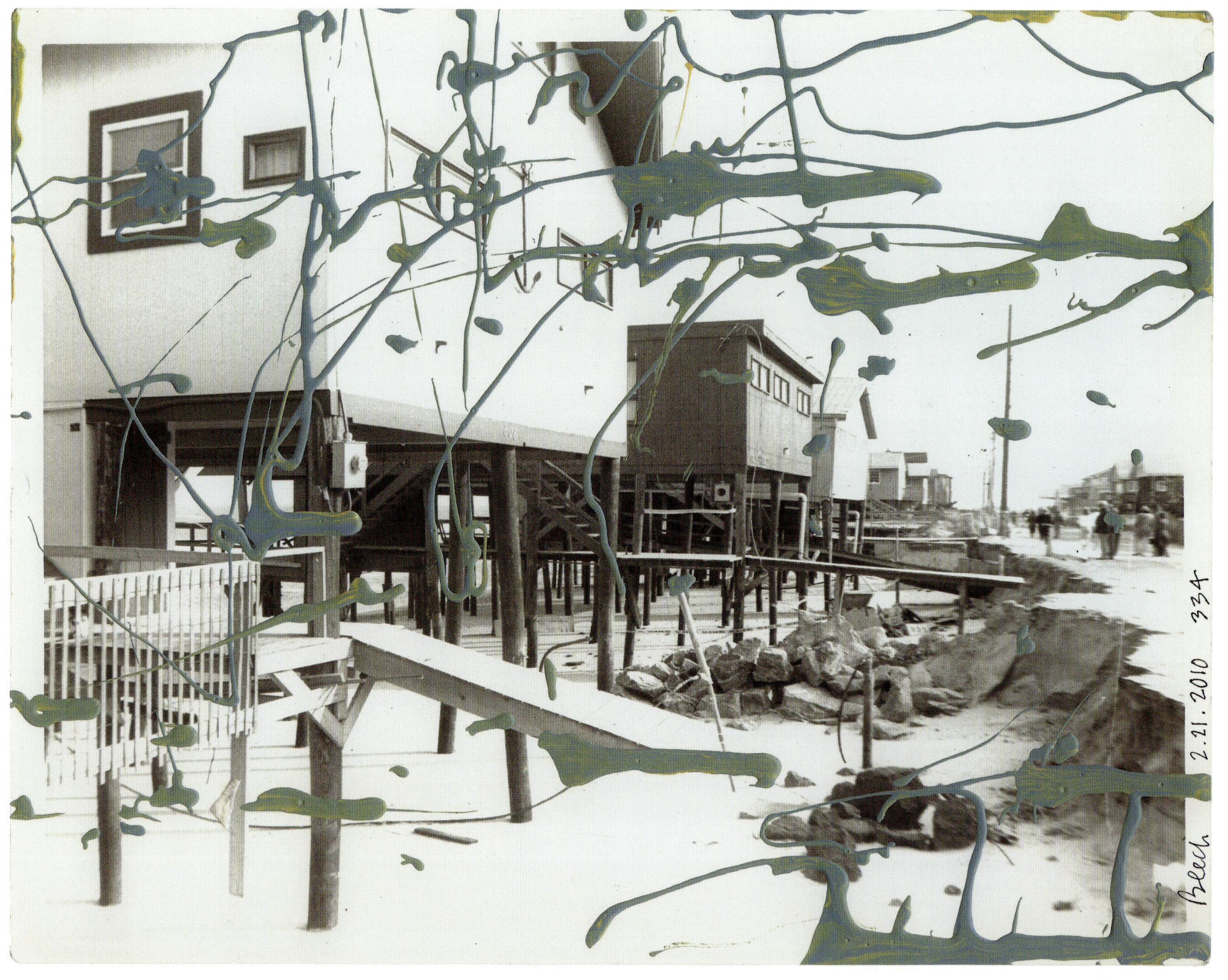

Beech   2.21.2010   334

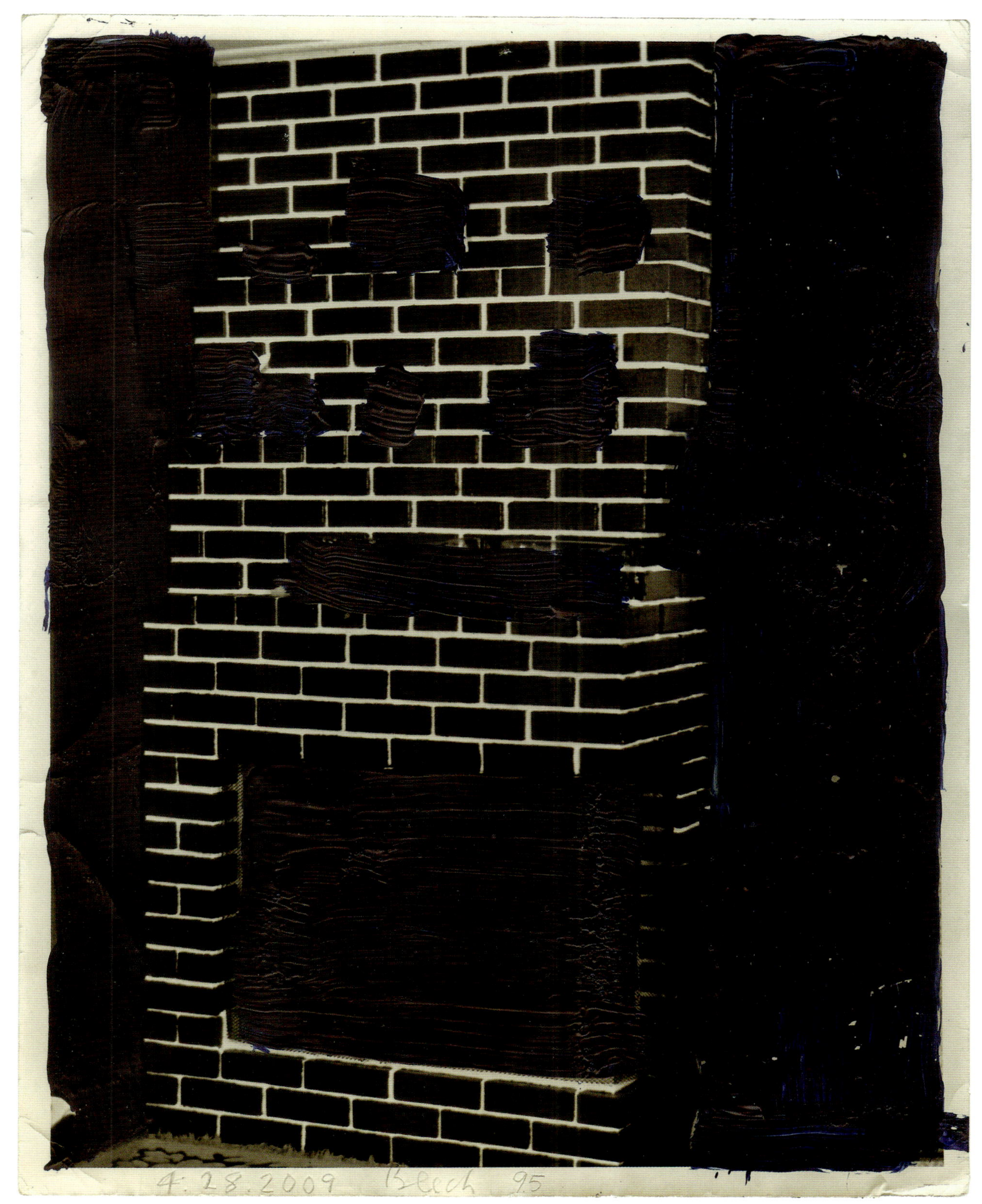

49

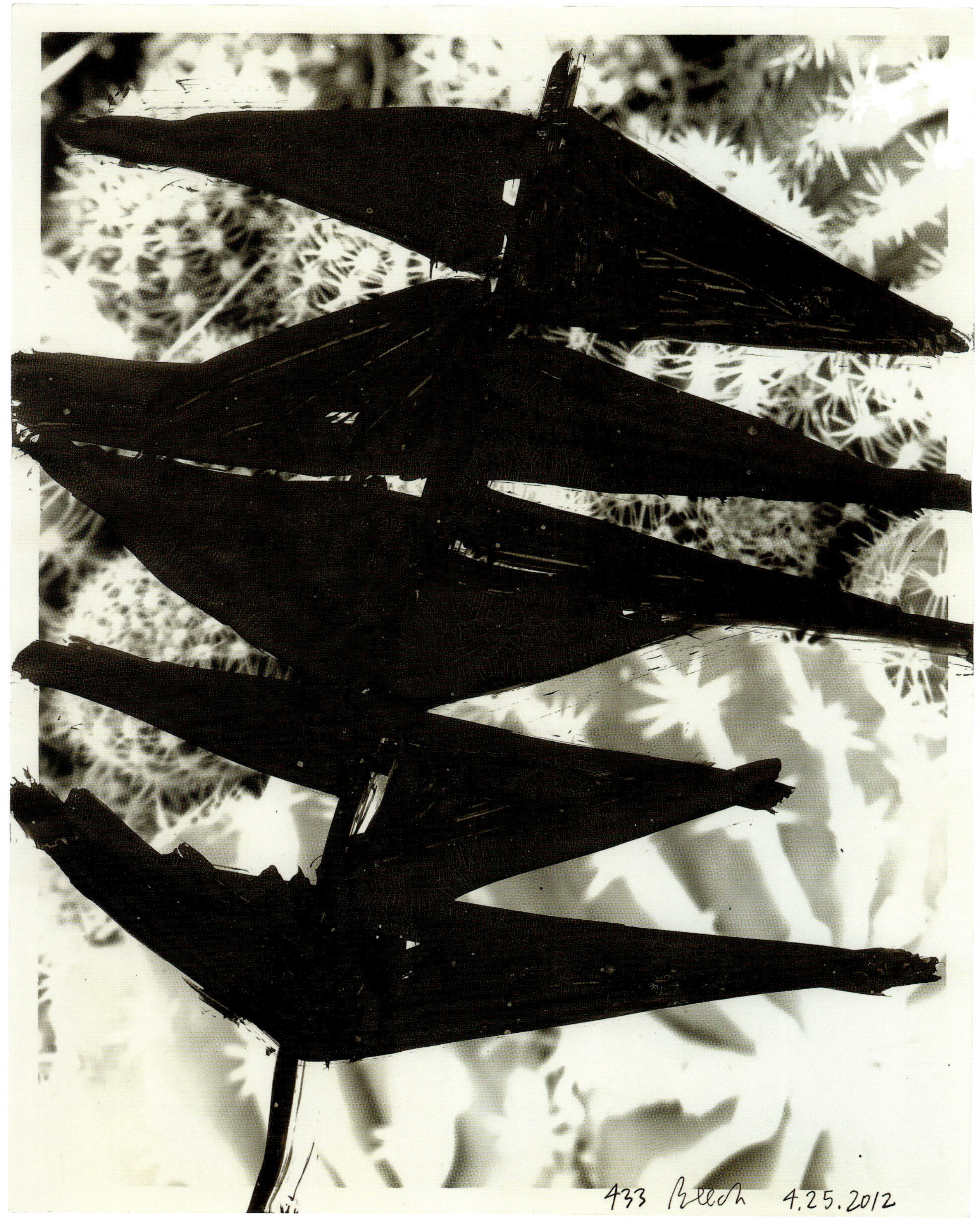
433 Bloch 4.25.2012

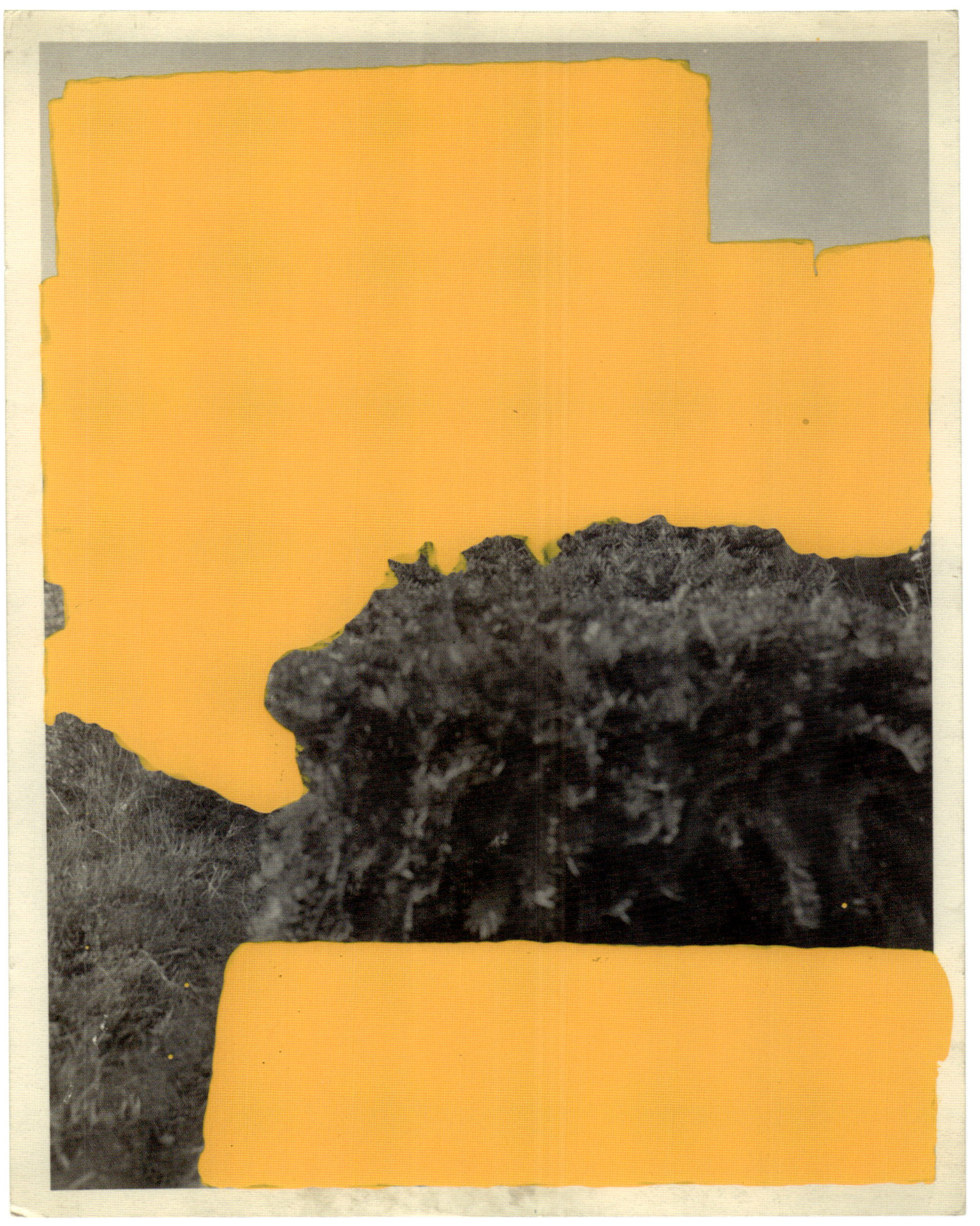

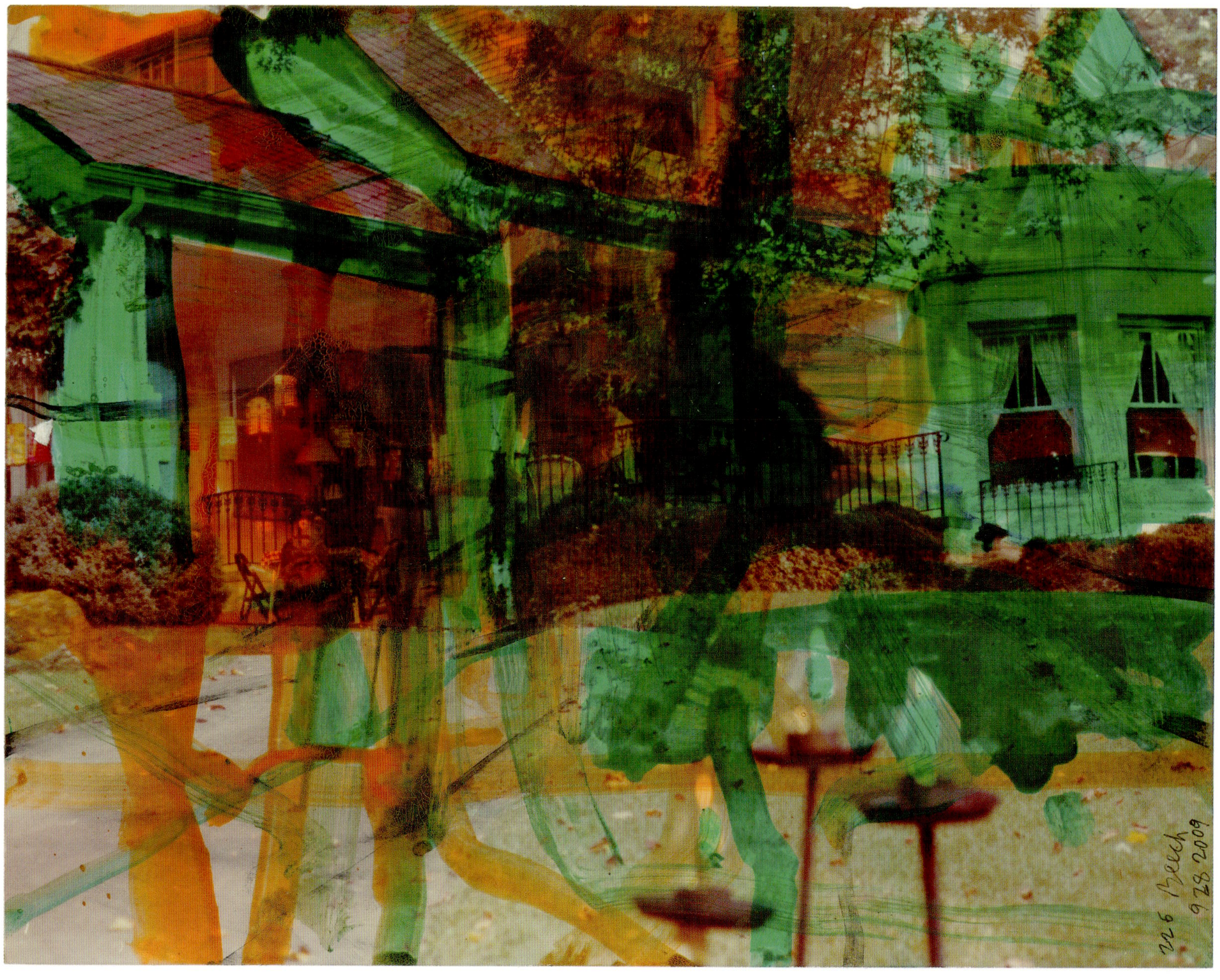
226 Beech
9 28 2009

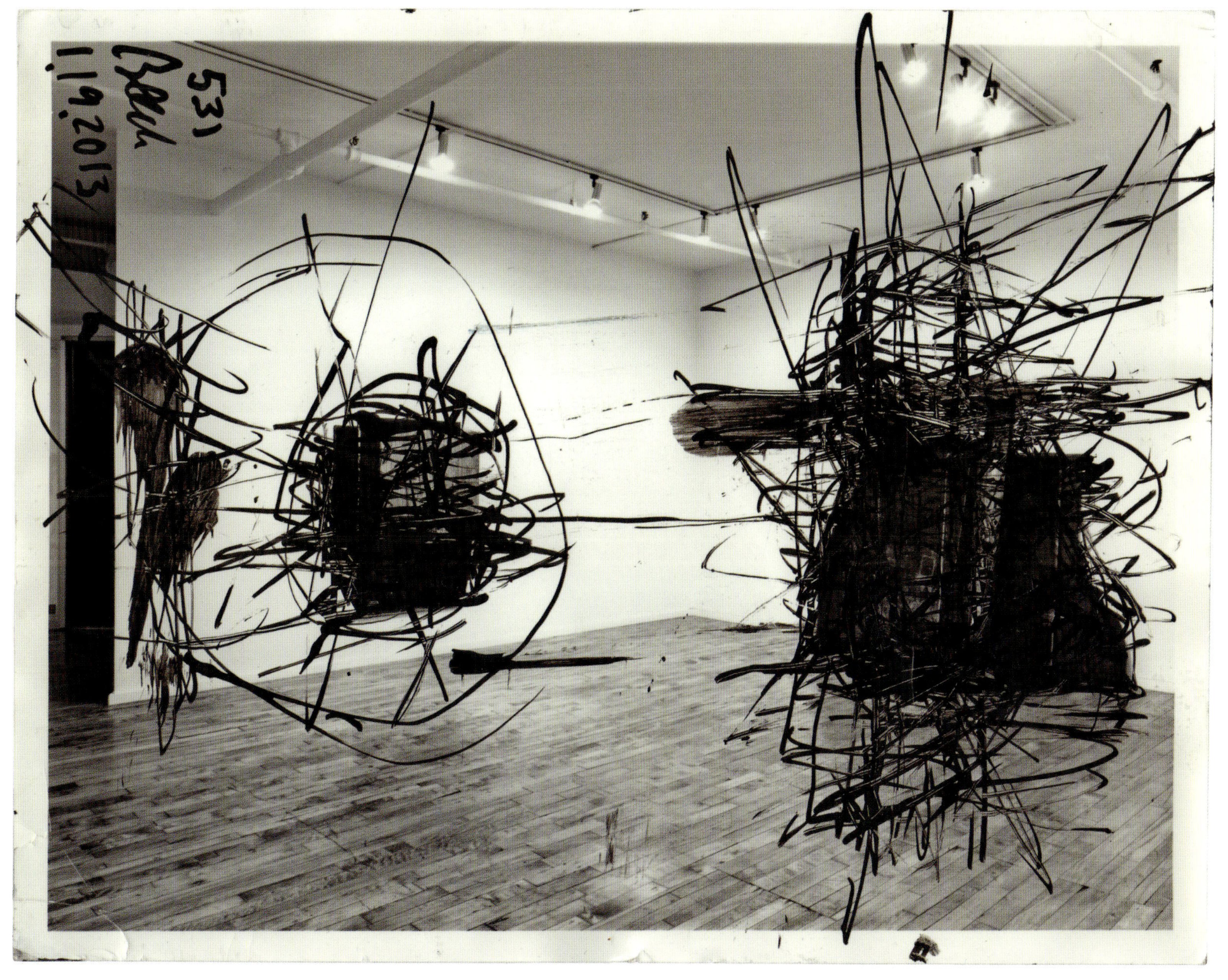

531
Beech
1.19.2013

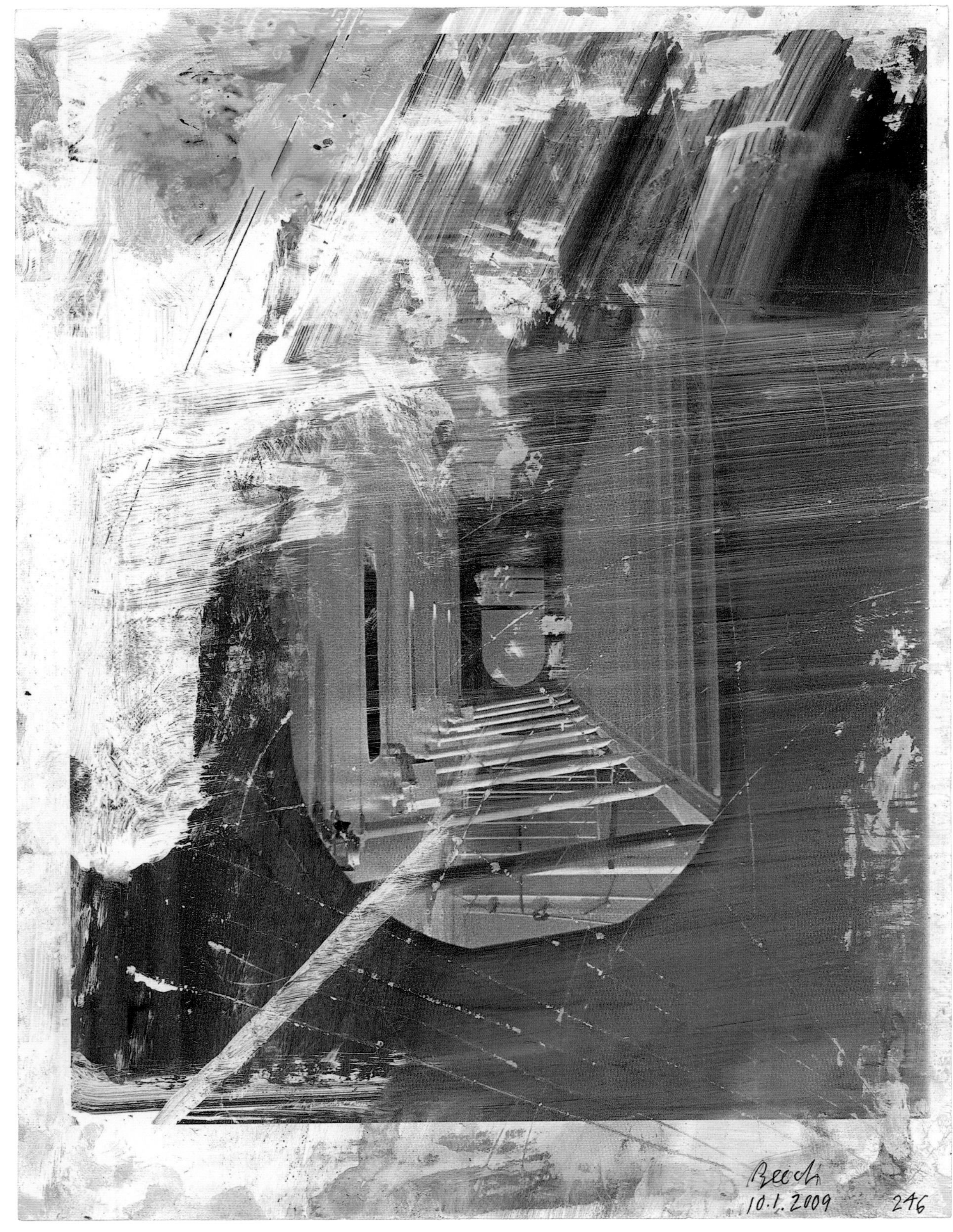
Beech
10.1.2009
246

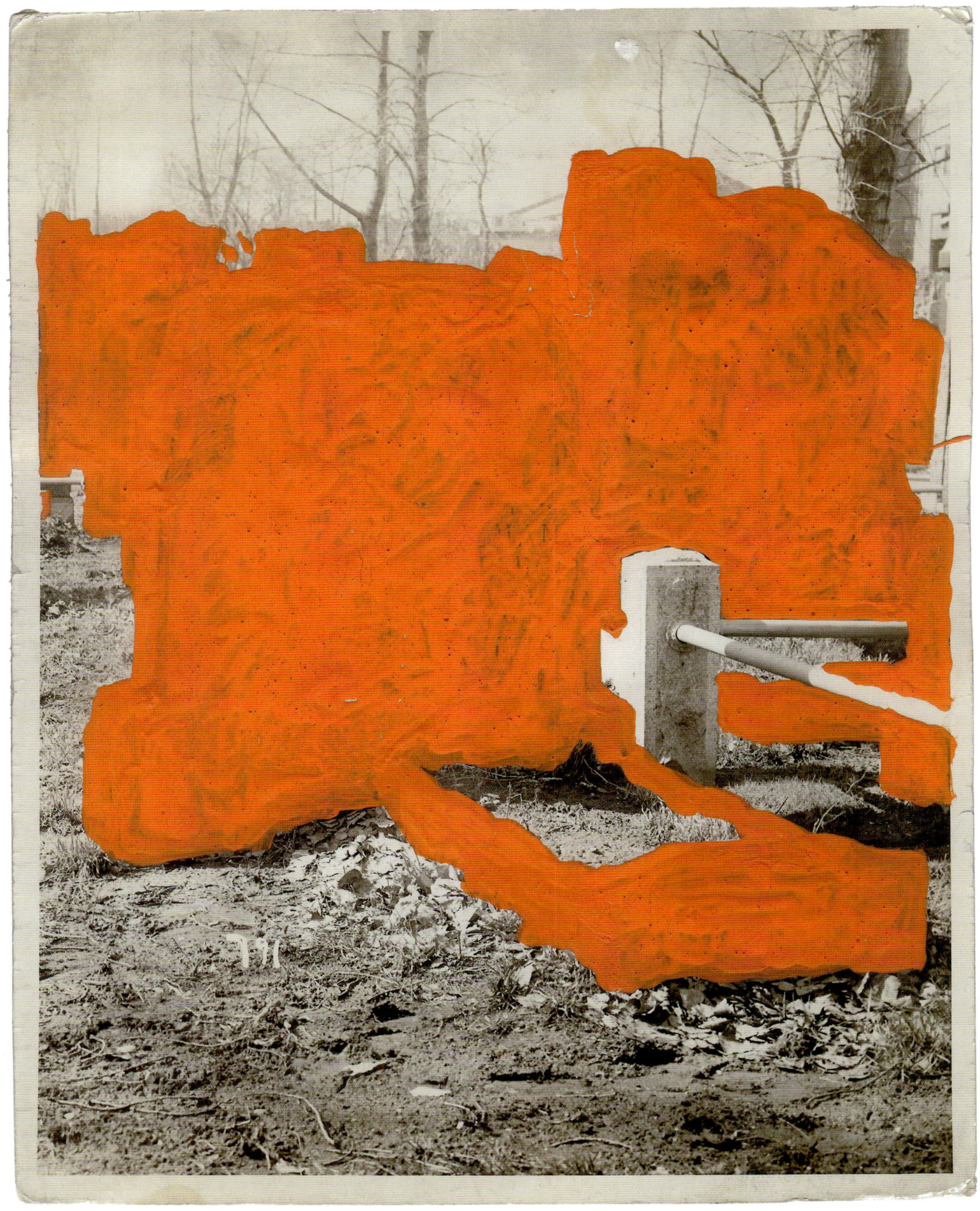

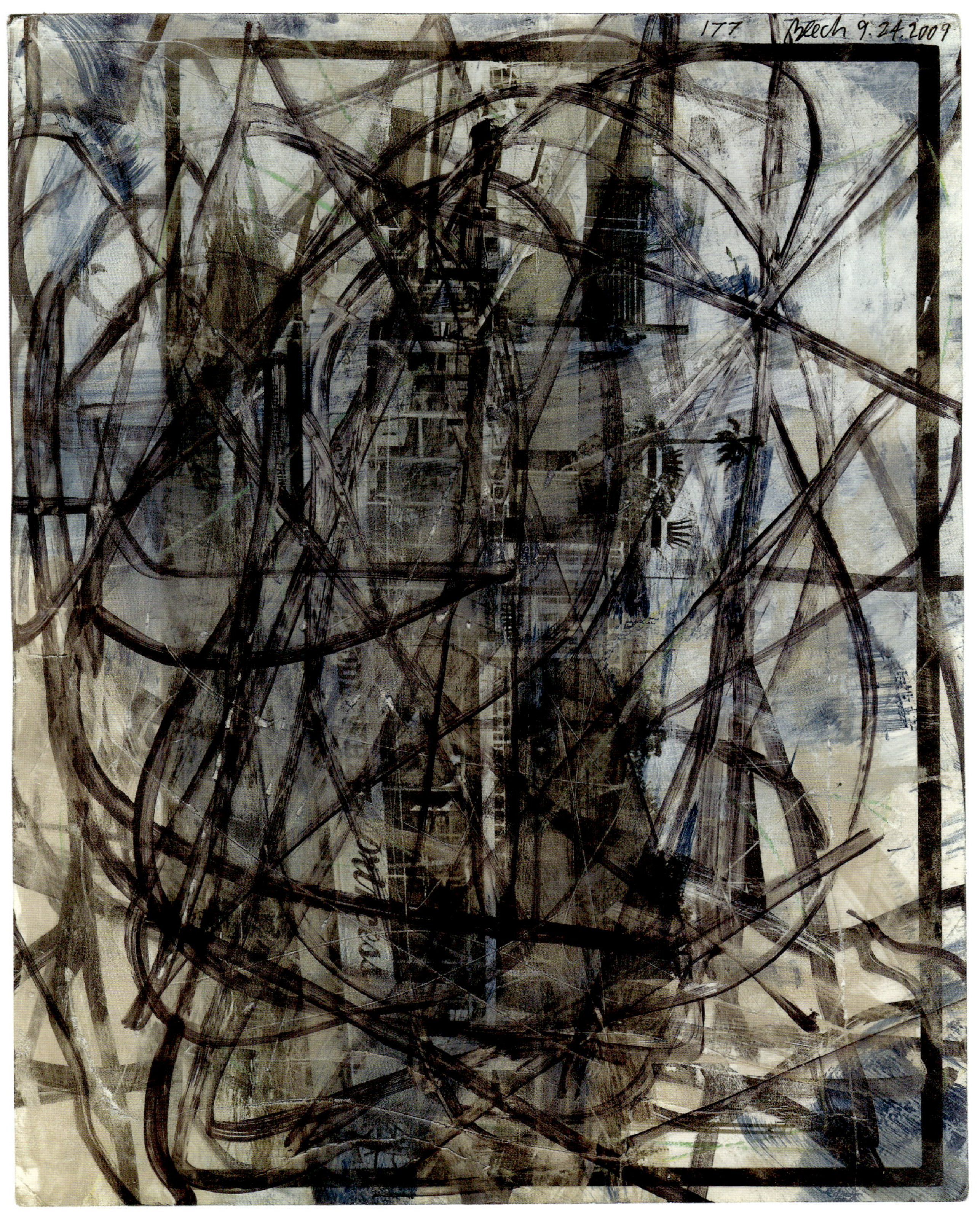

177   Blech 9.24.2009

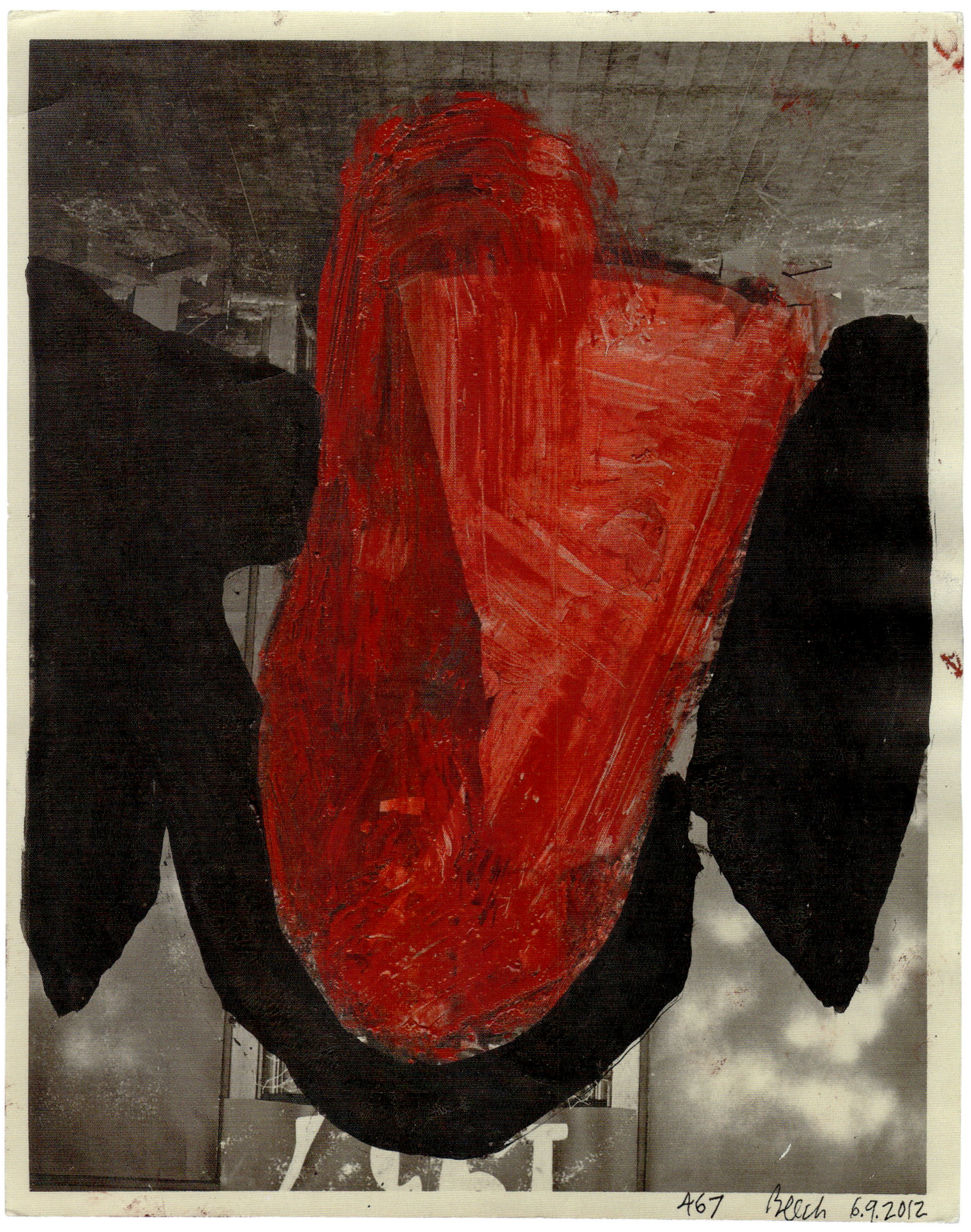

467   Blech 6.9.2012

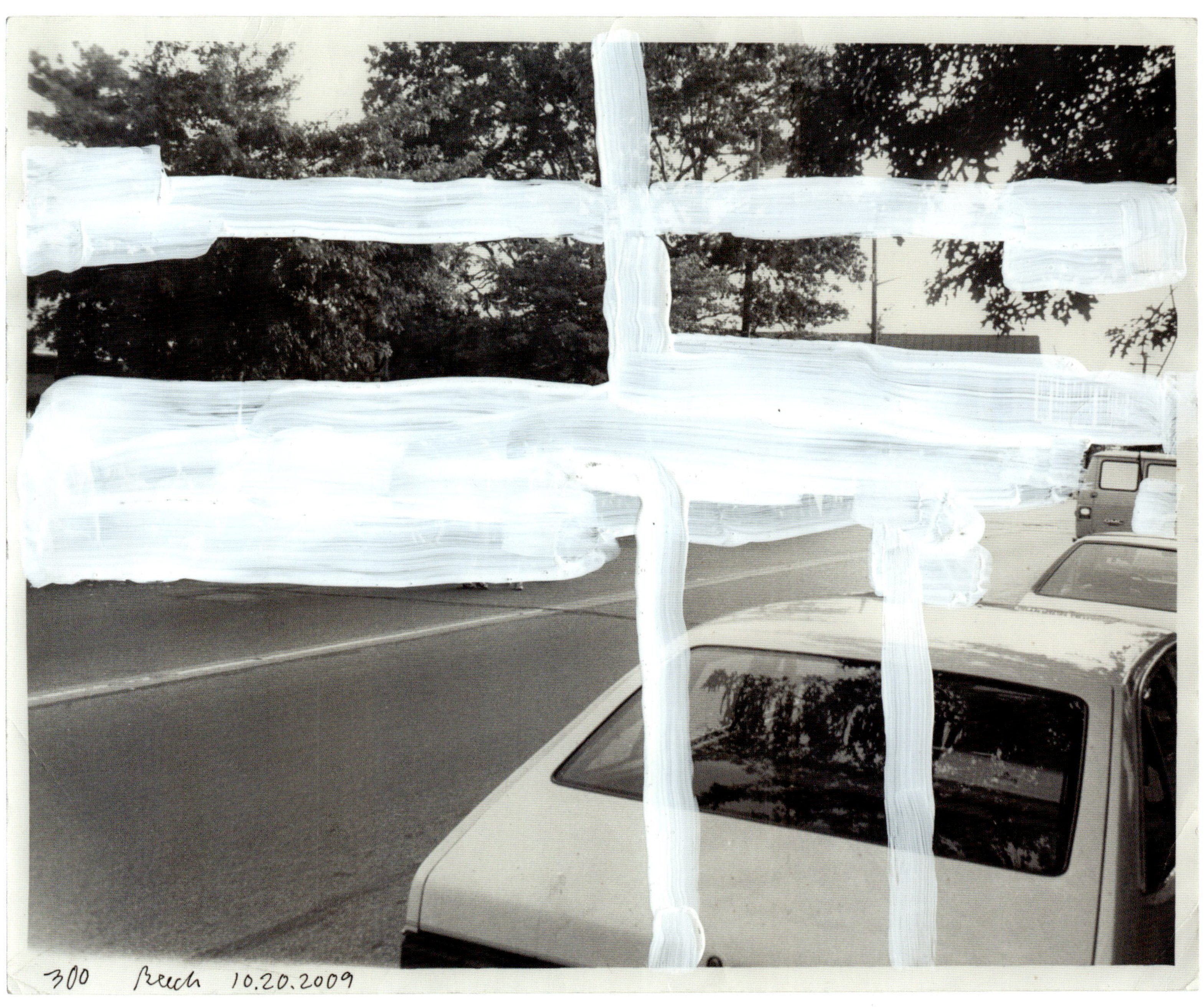

59

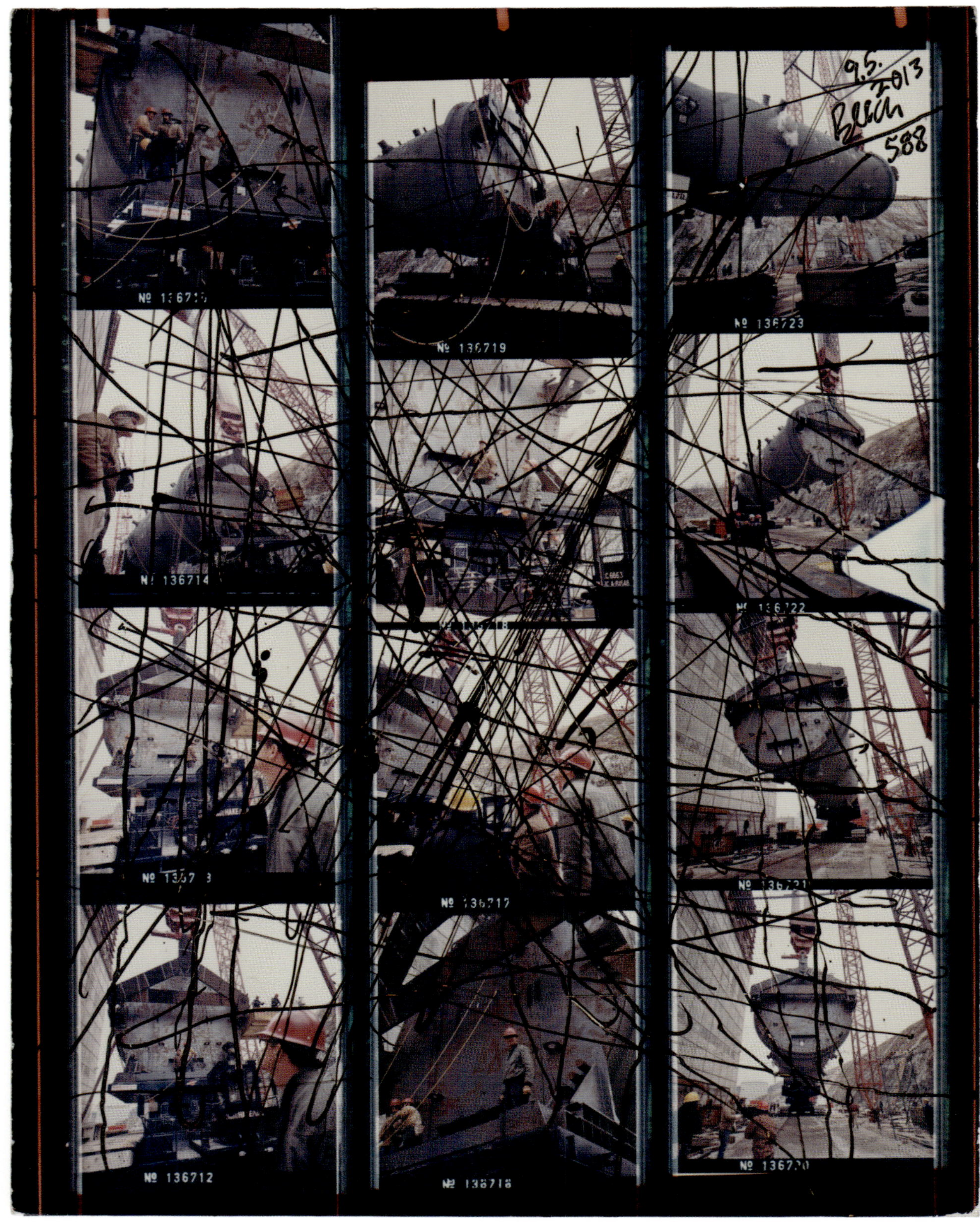

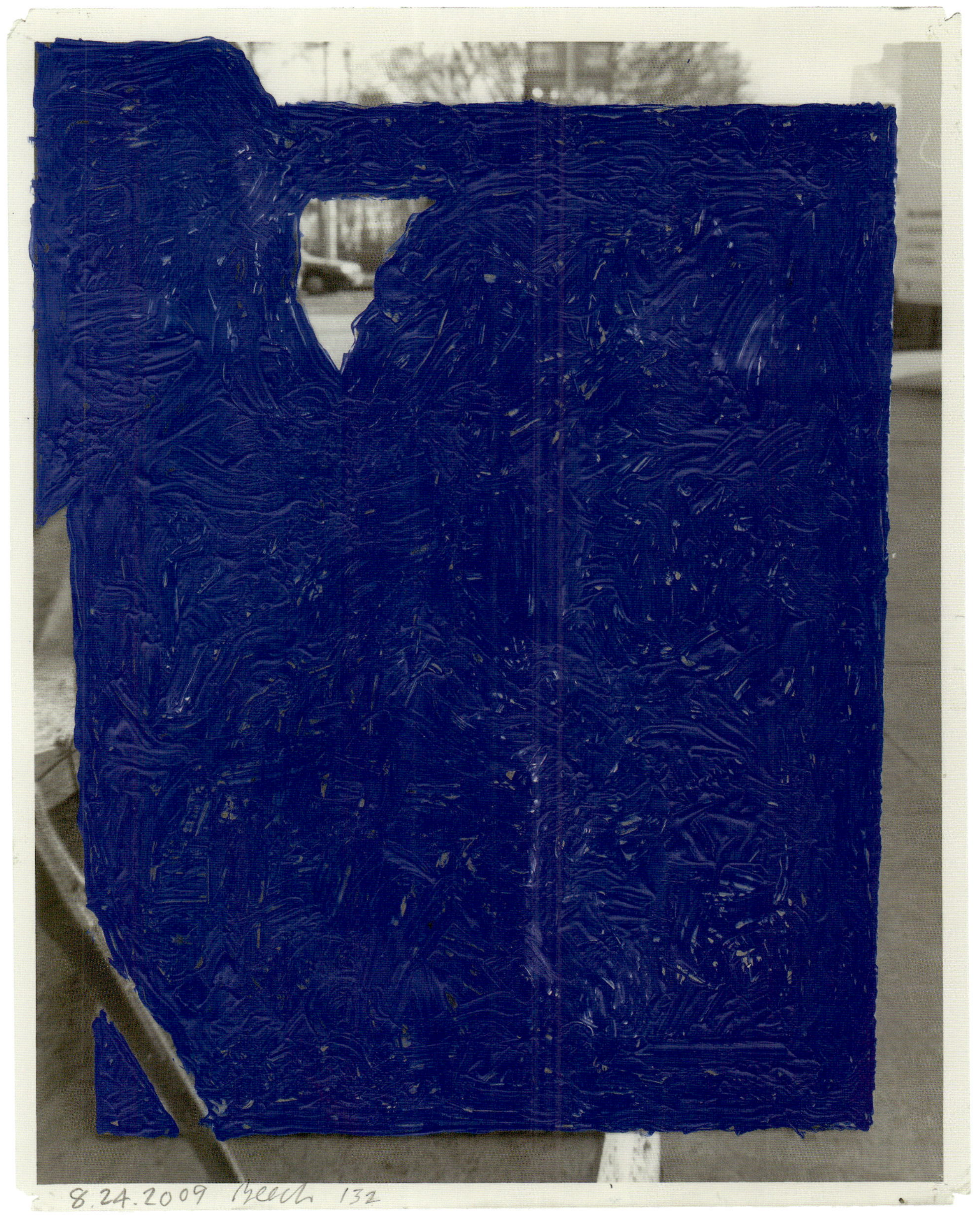
8.24.2009 Beech 132

570
Beech
5.23.2013
Hudson, N.Y

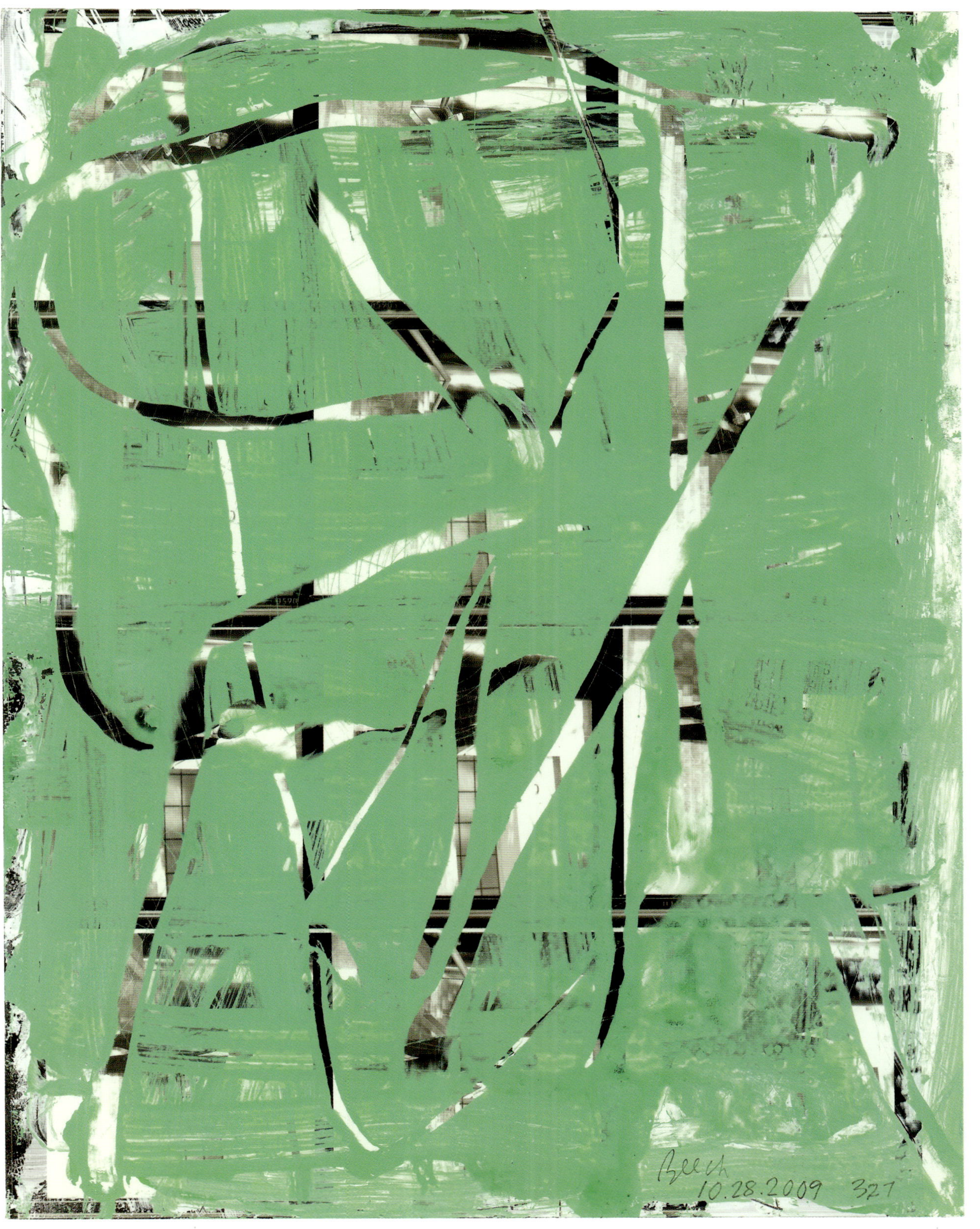

Bech
10.28.2009   327

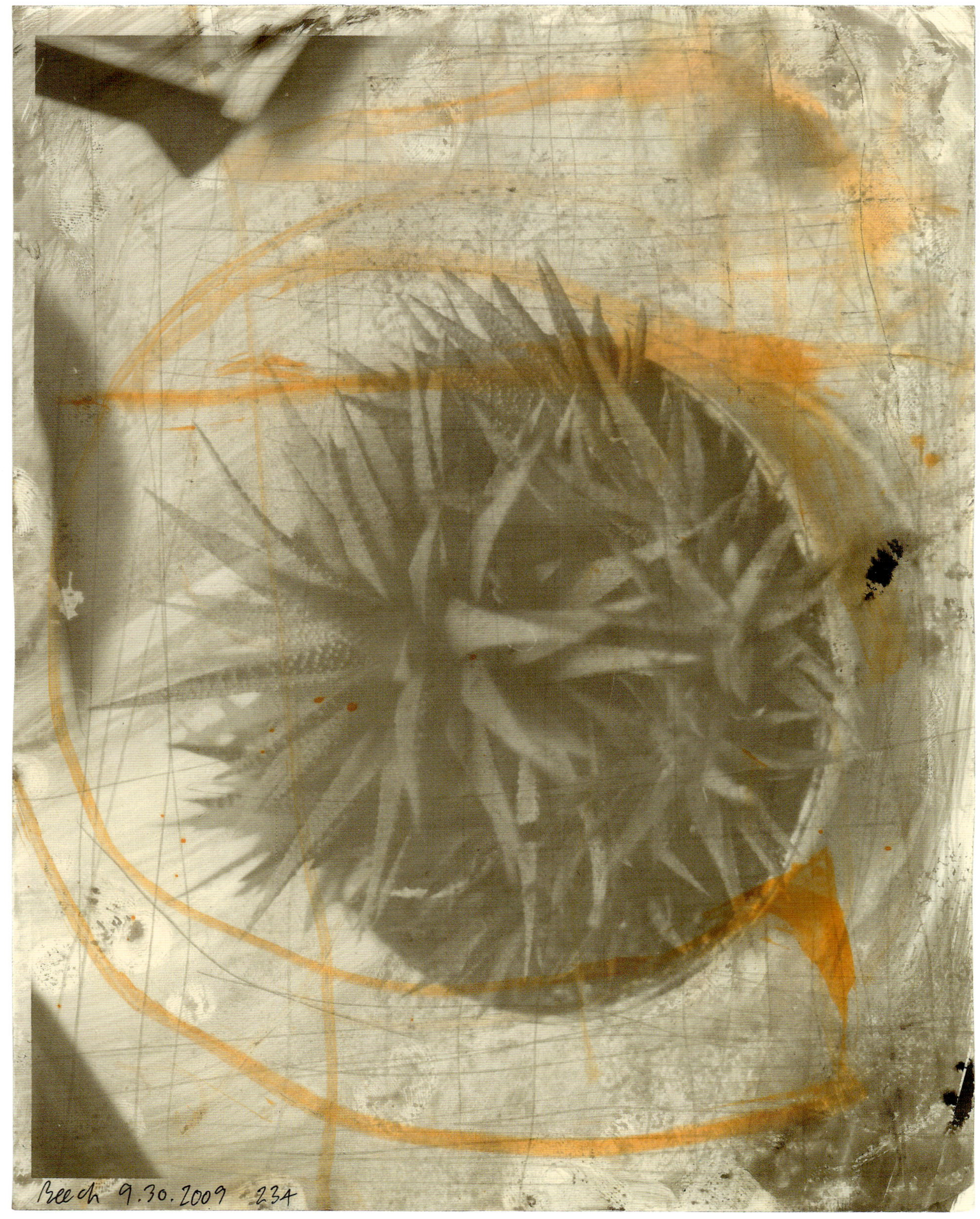
Beech 9.30.2009 234

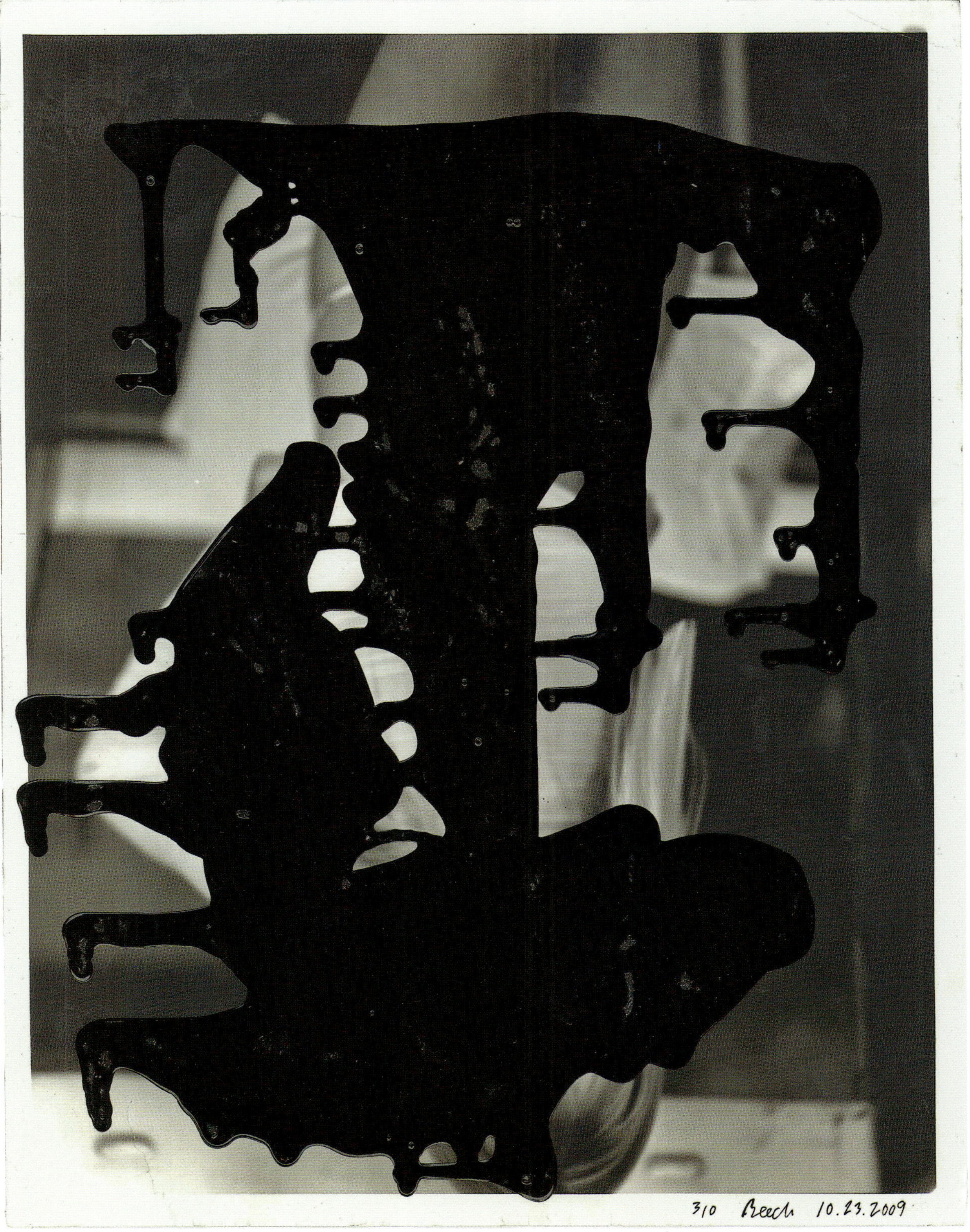

3/0   Beech   10.23.2009

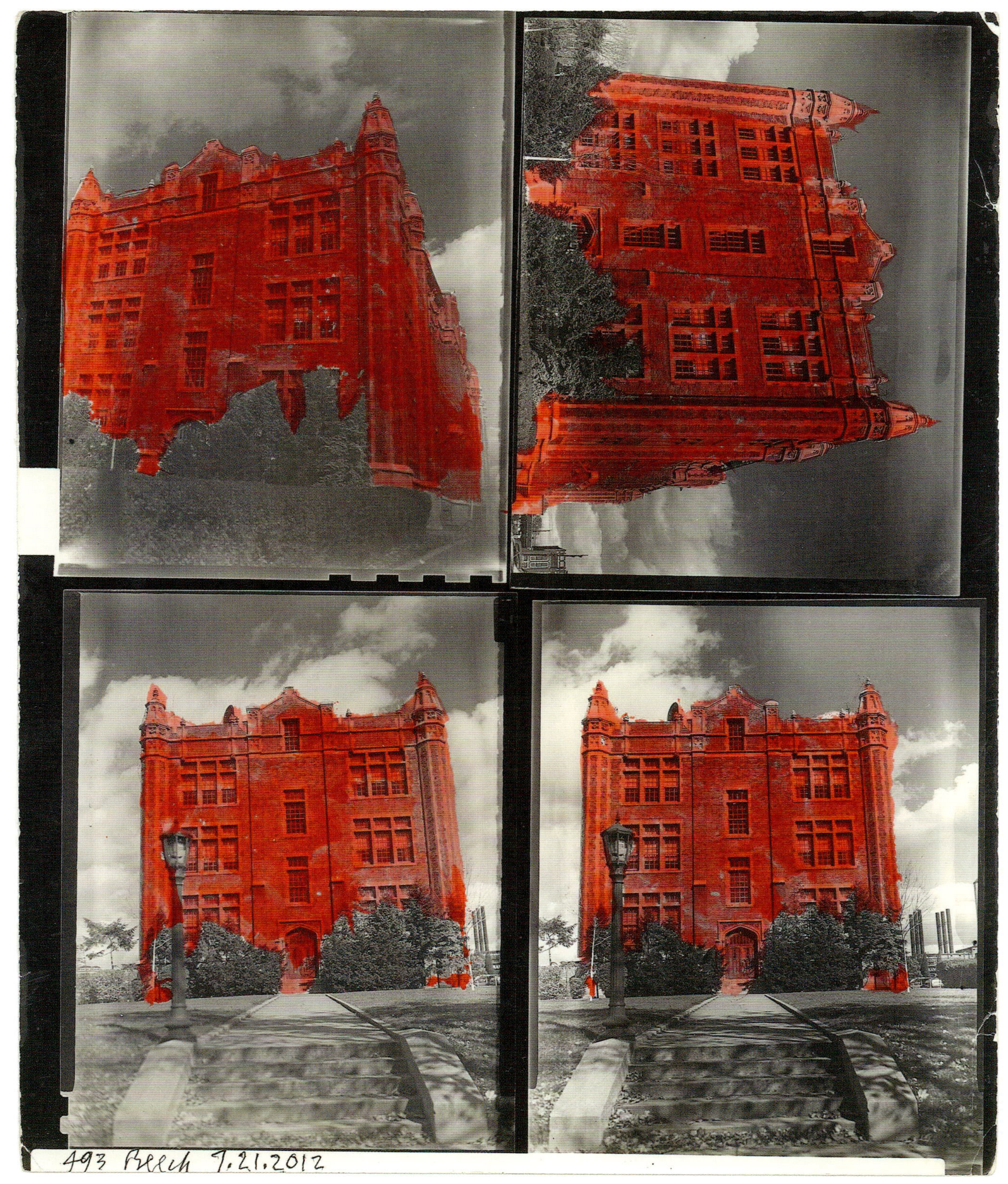

493 Beech 9.21.2012

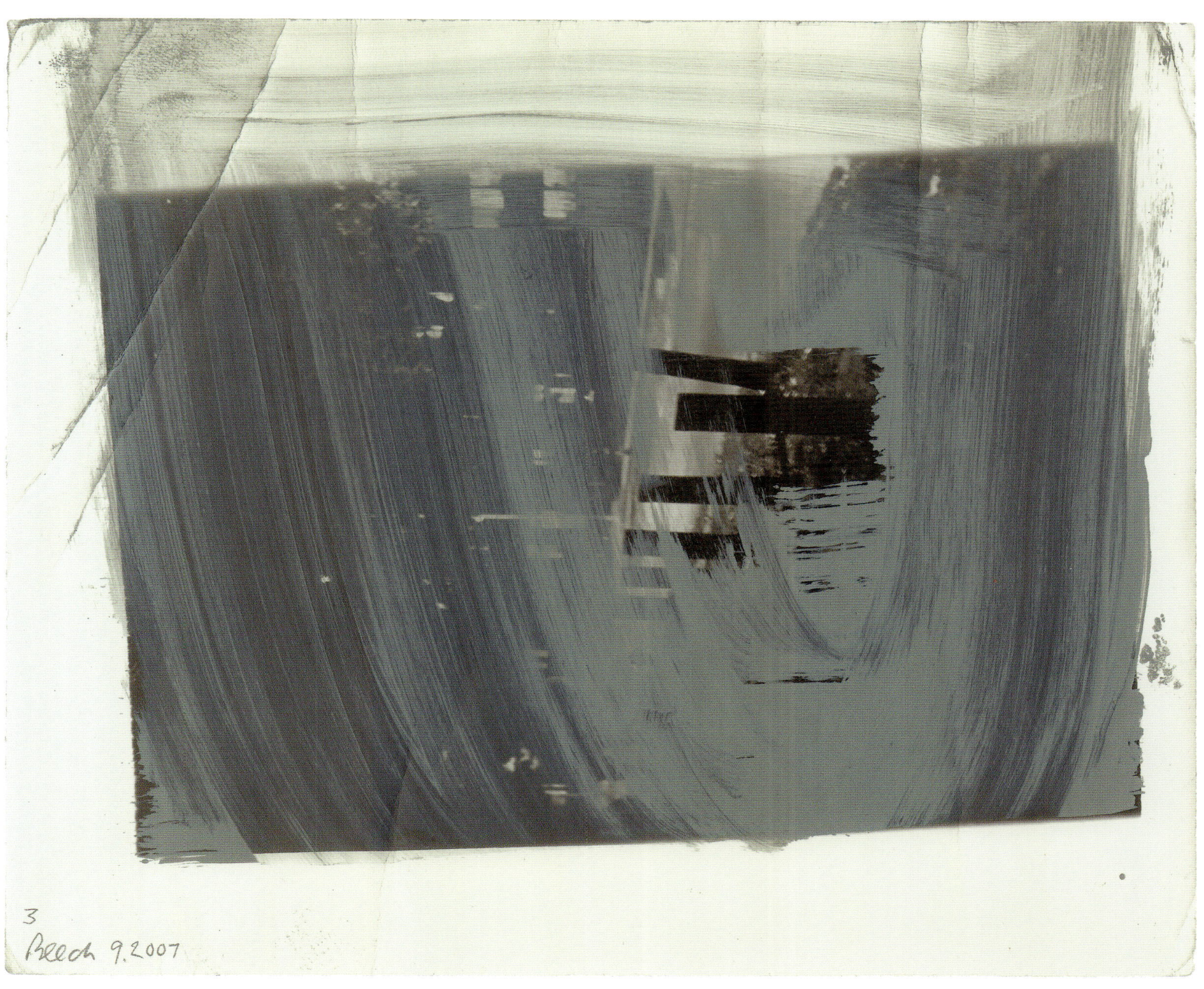

3
Blech 9.2007

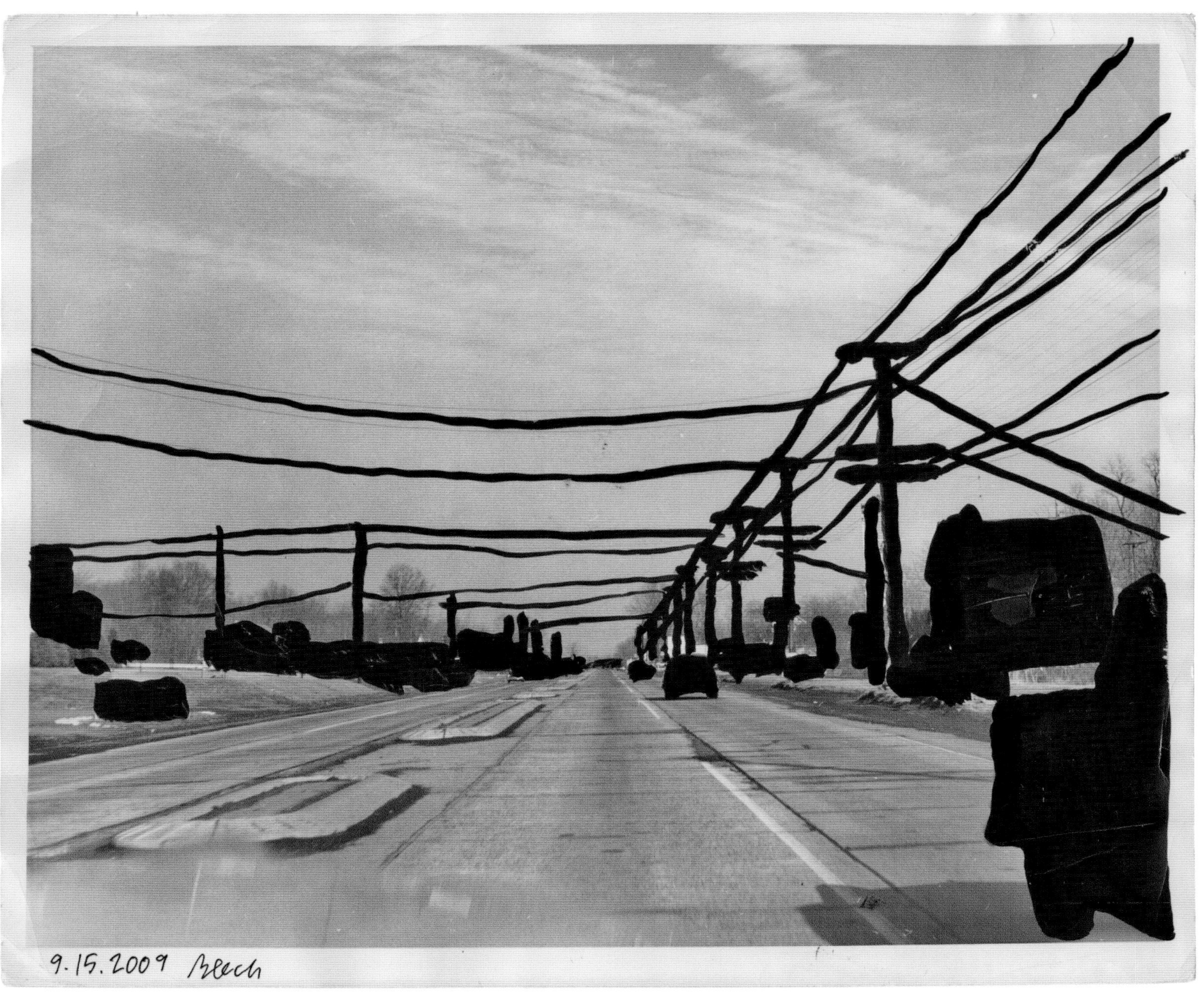

9.15.2009 Beech

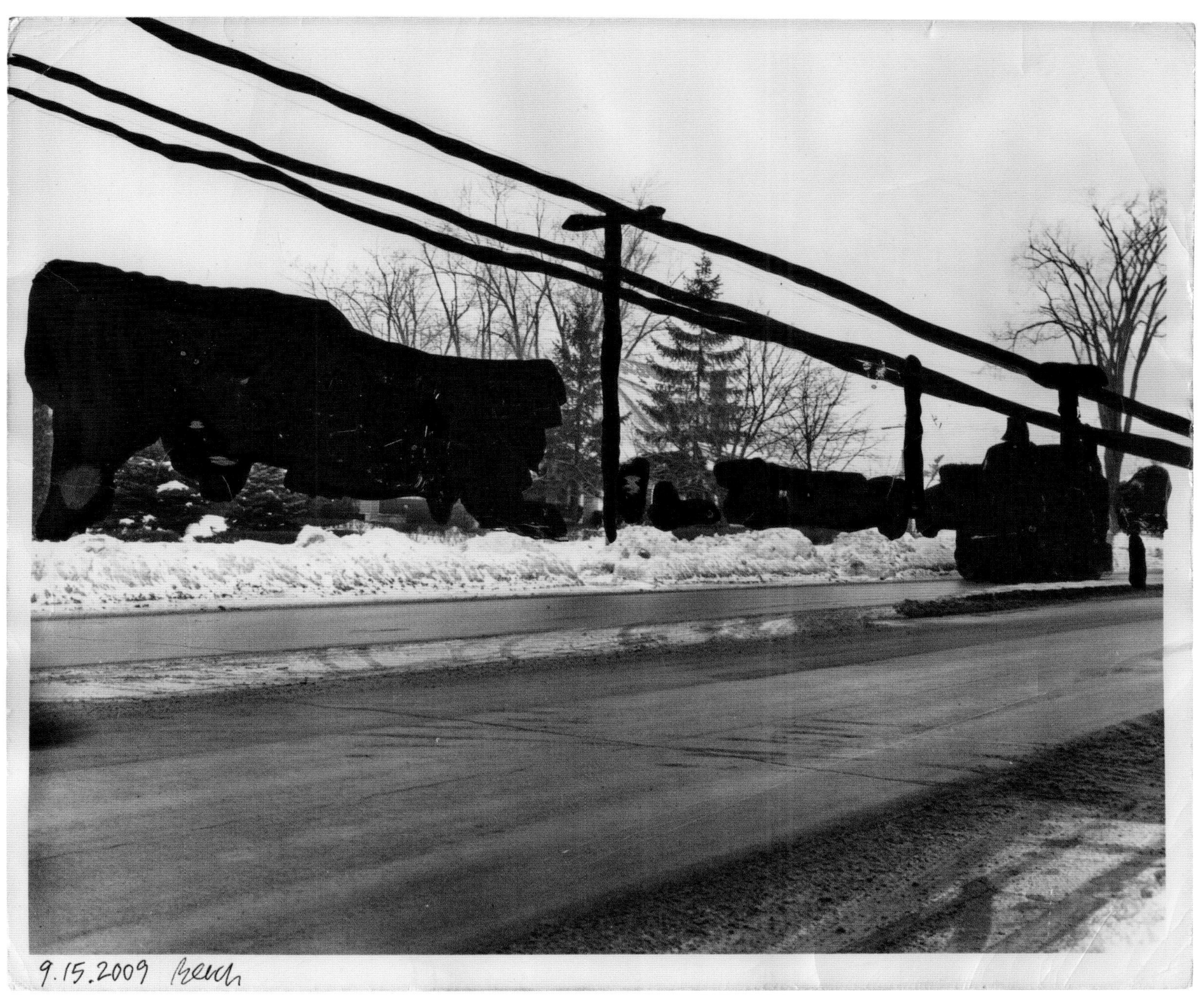

9.15.2009 Beach

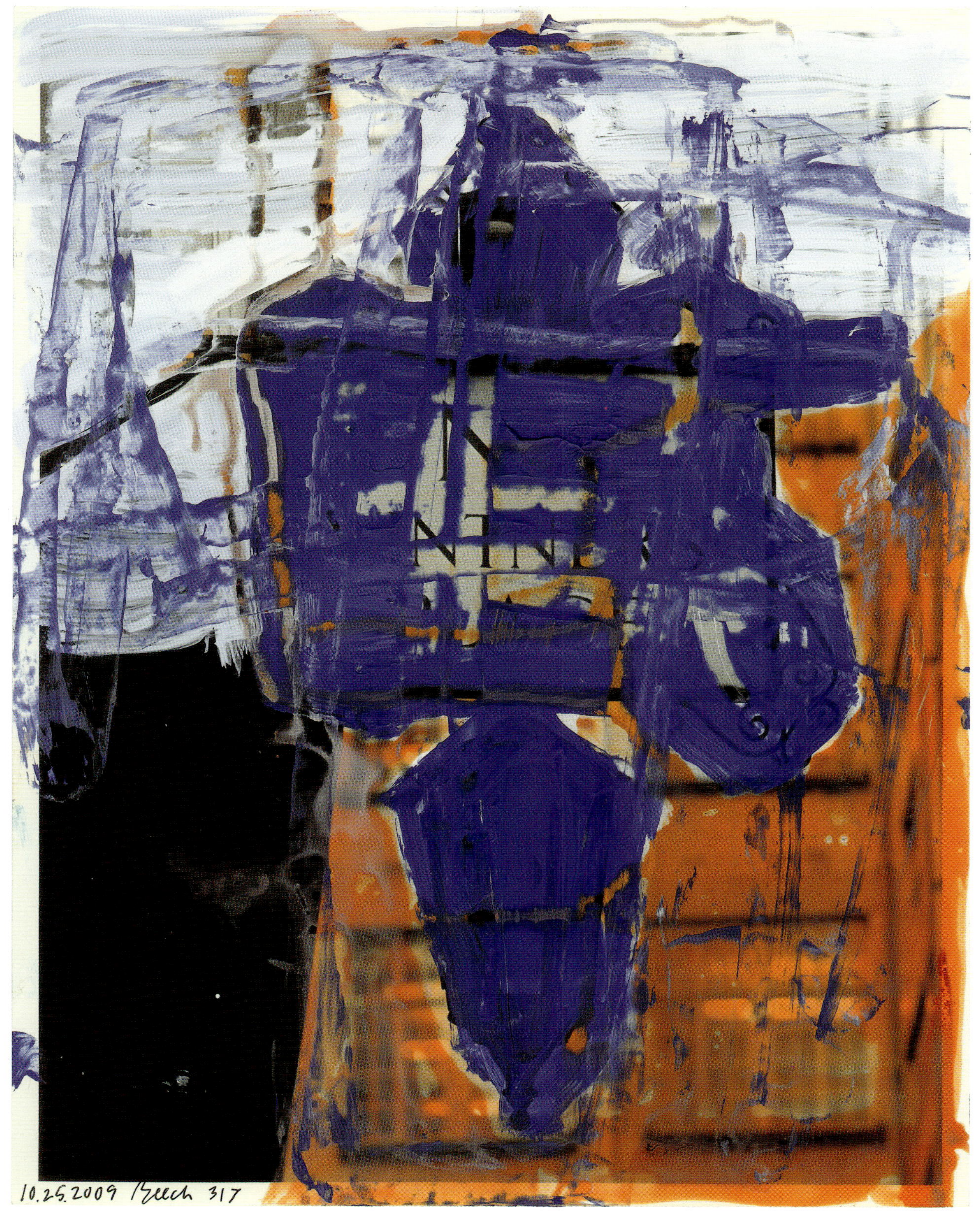
10.25.2009 Beech 317

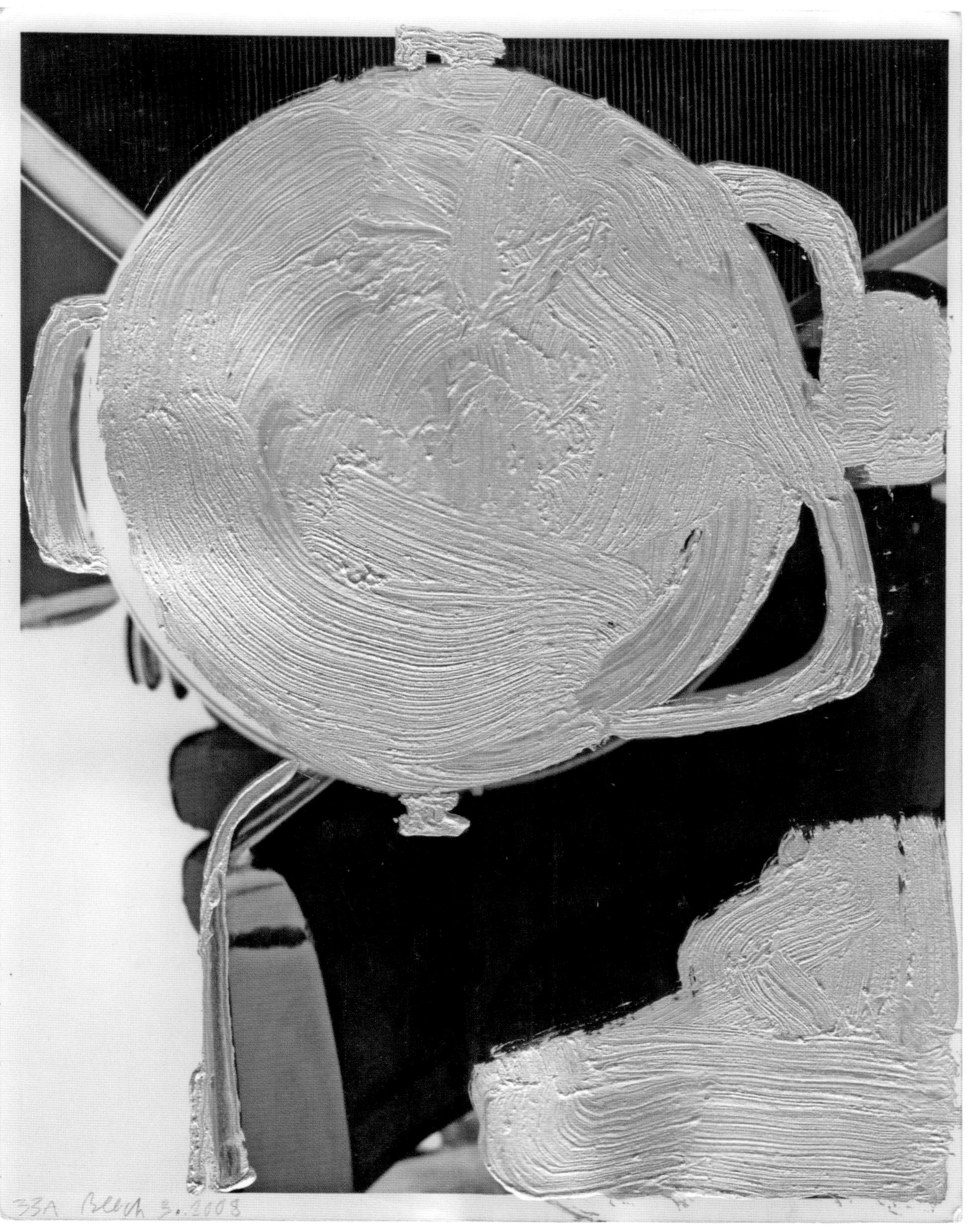
33A Blech 3. 2008

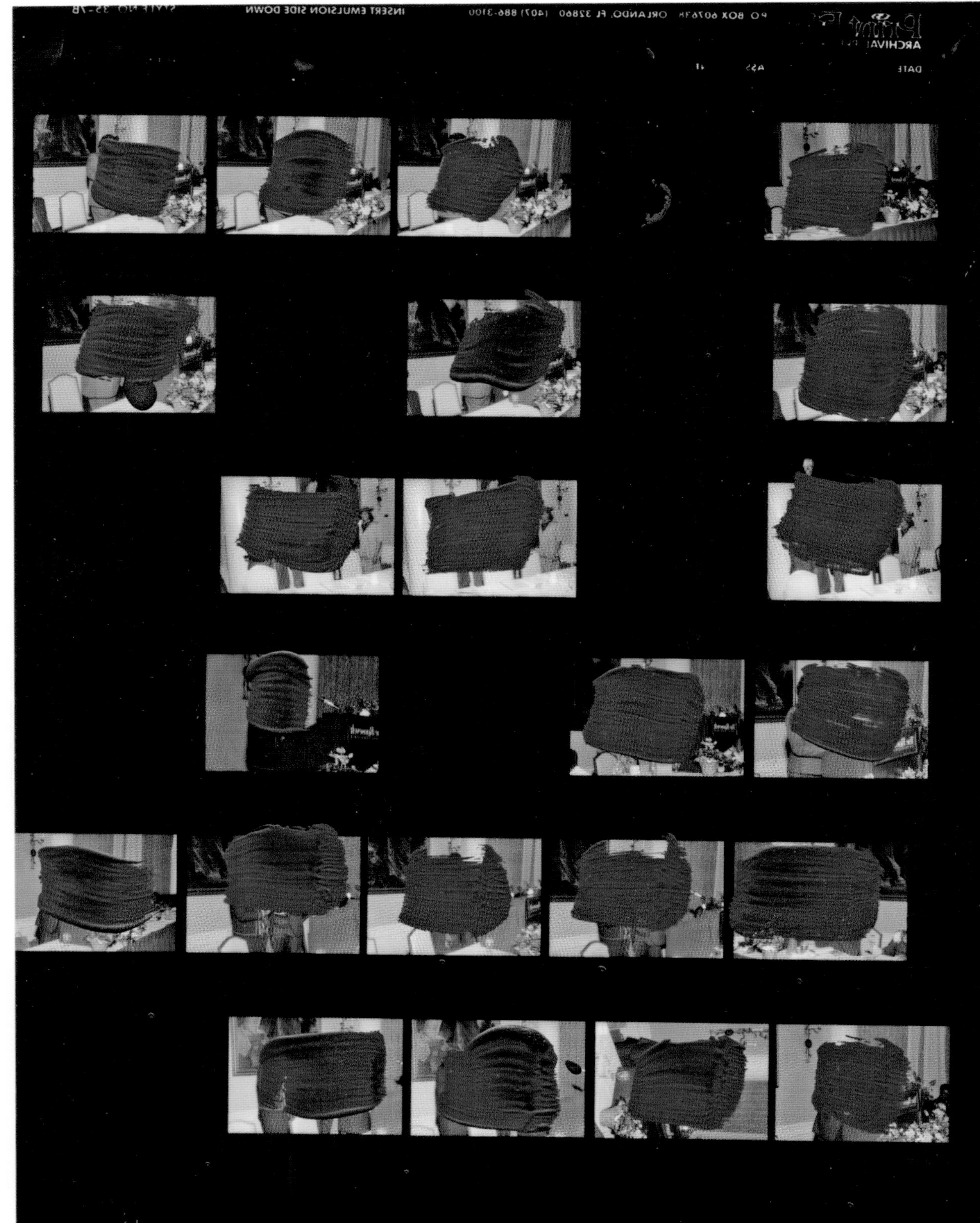

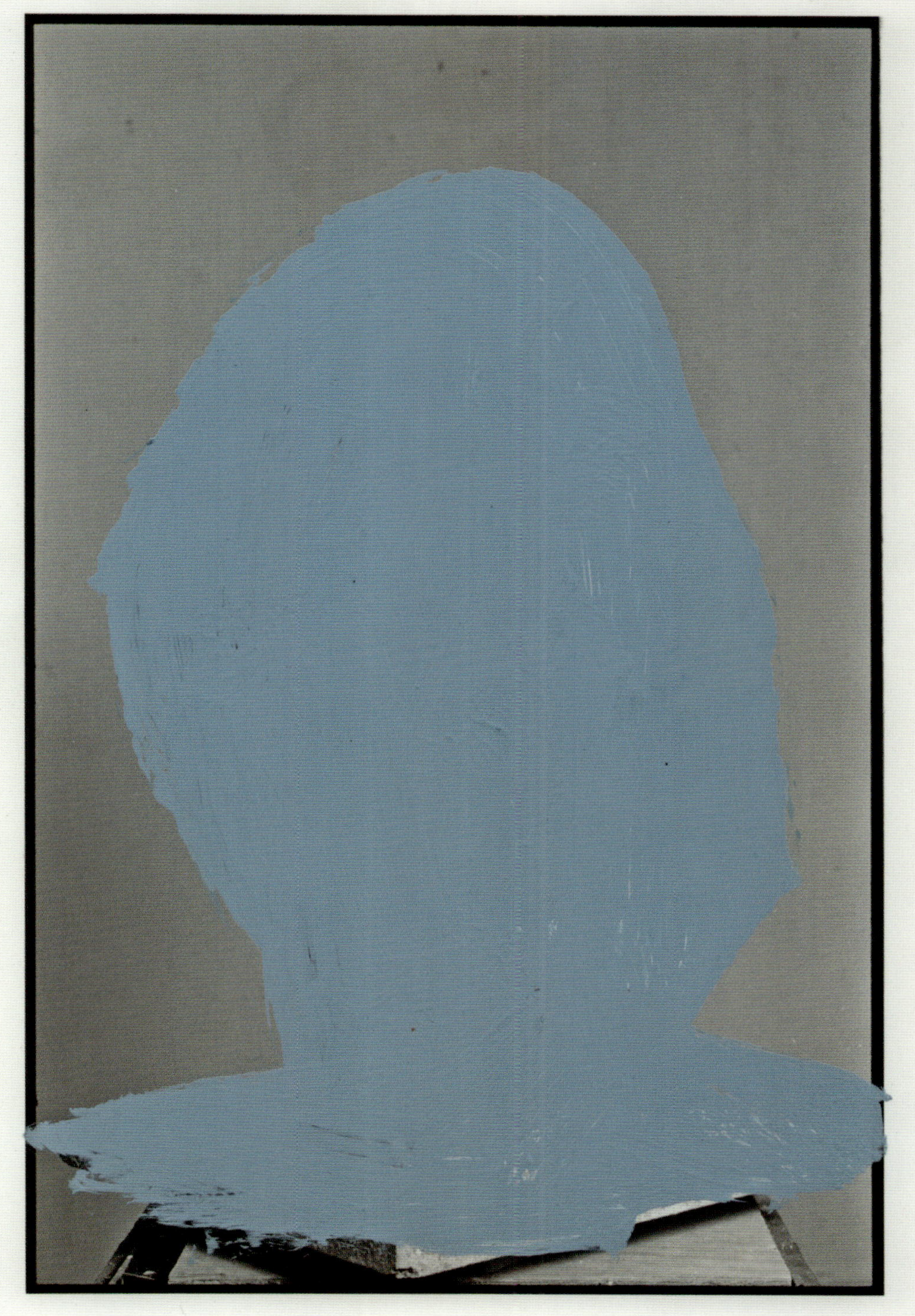

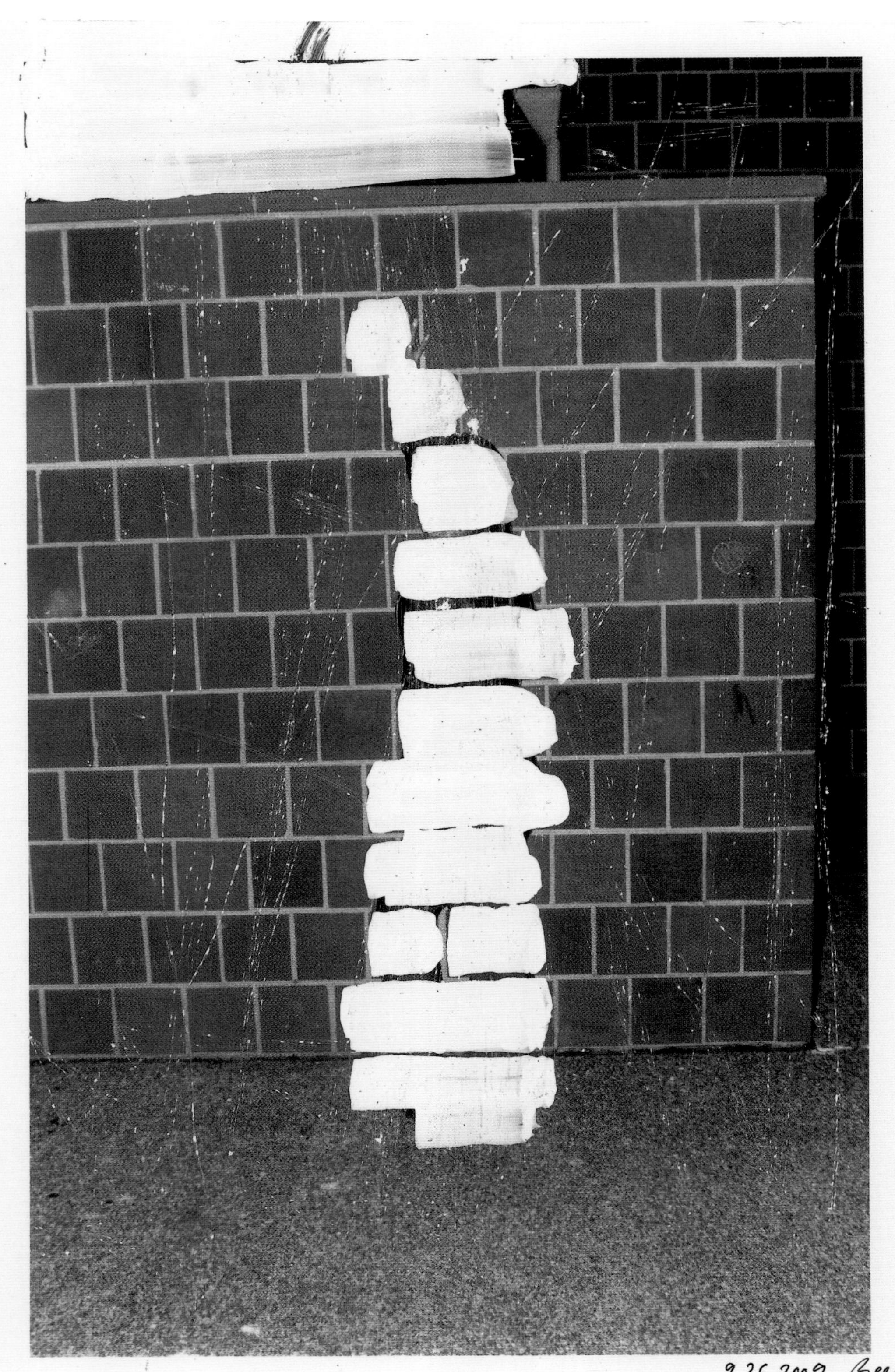

9.26.2009 Beech 196

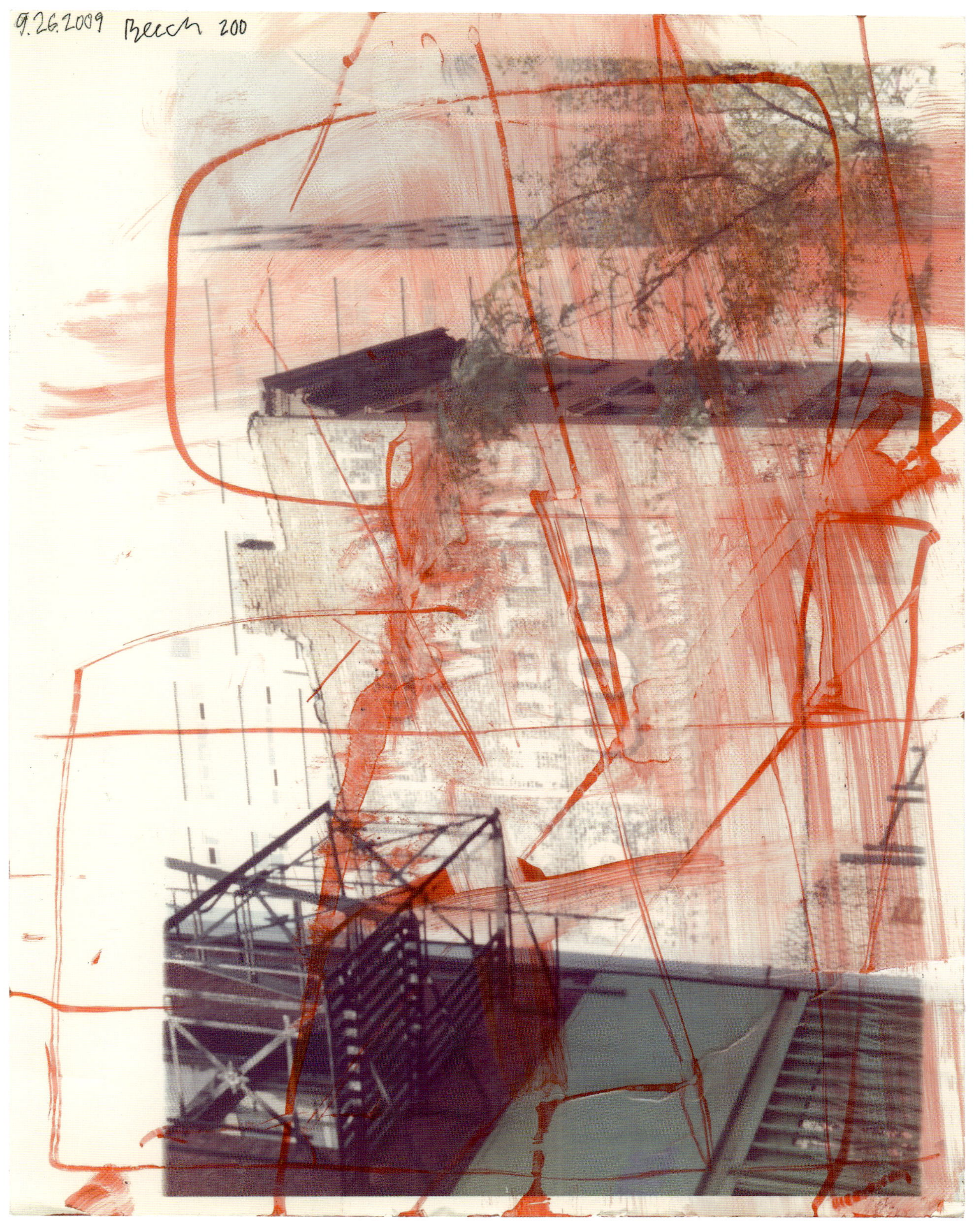
9.26.2009 Beech 200

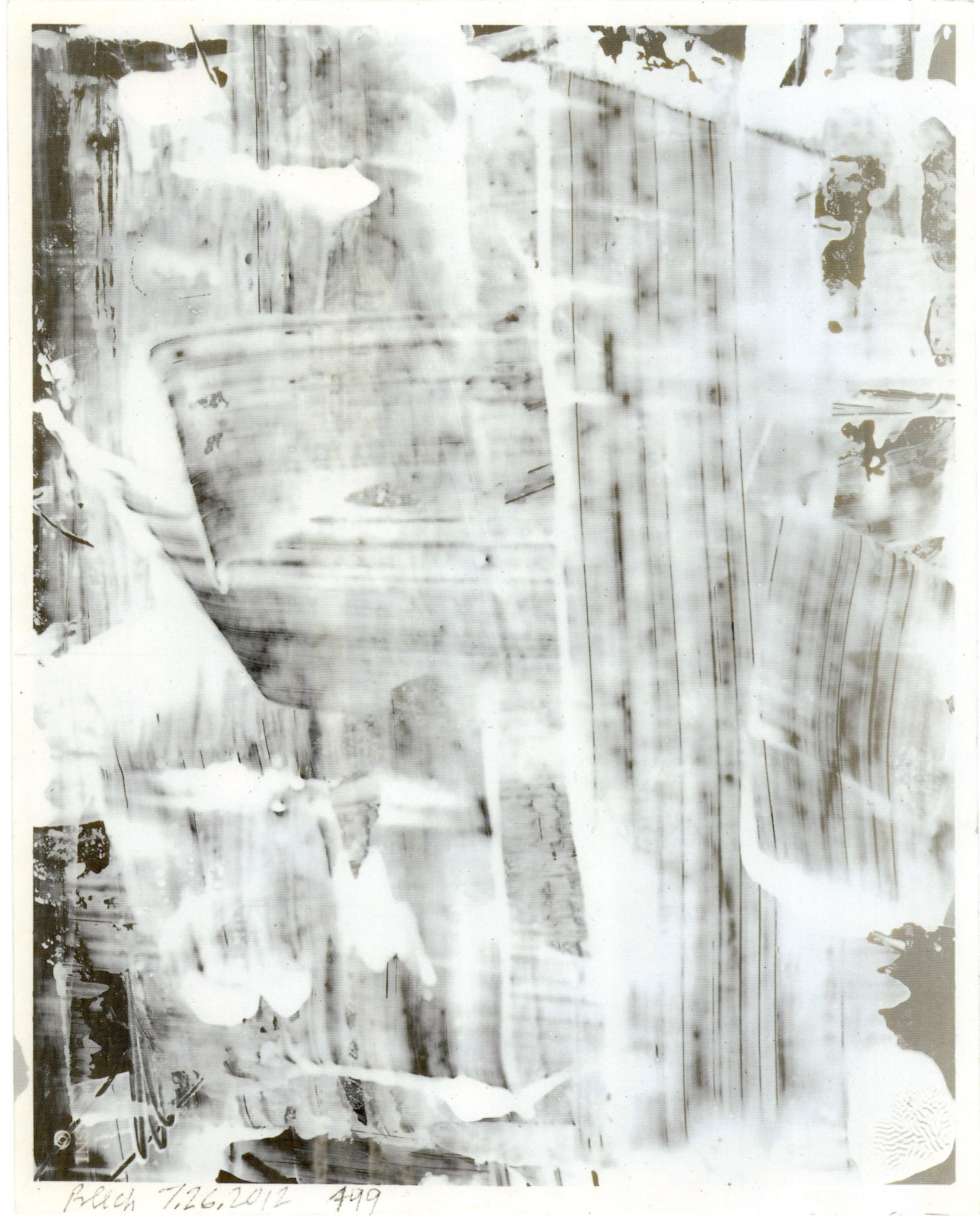

Bleach 7.26.2012   499

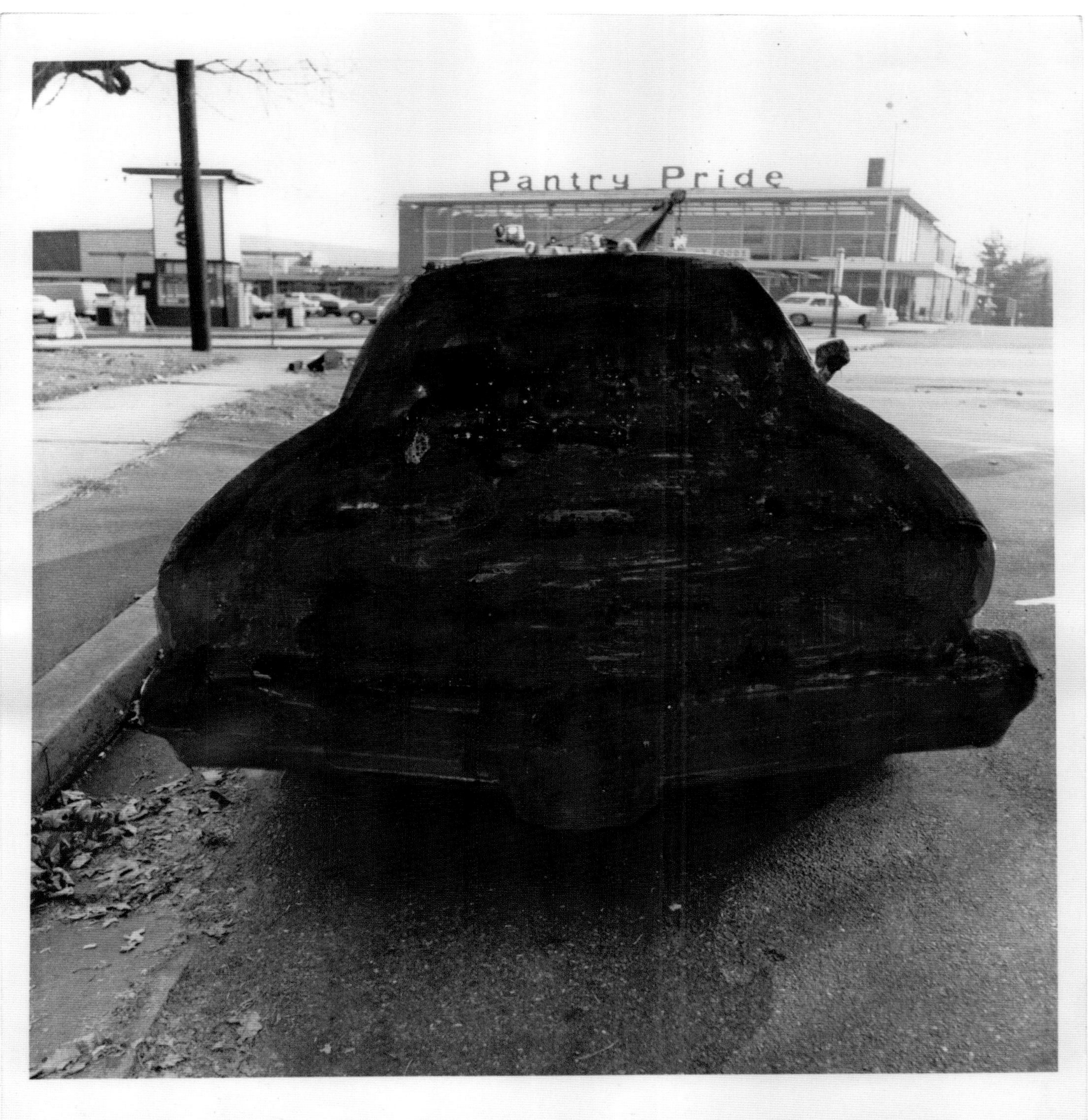

491 Beech 7.21.2012

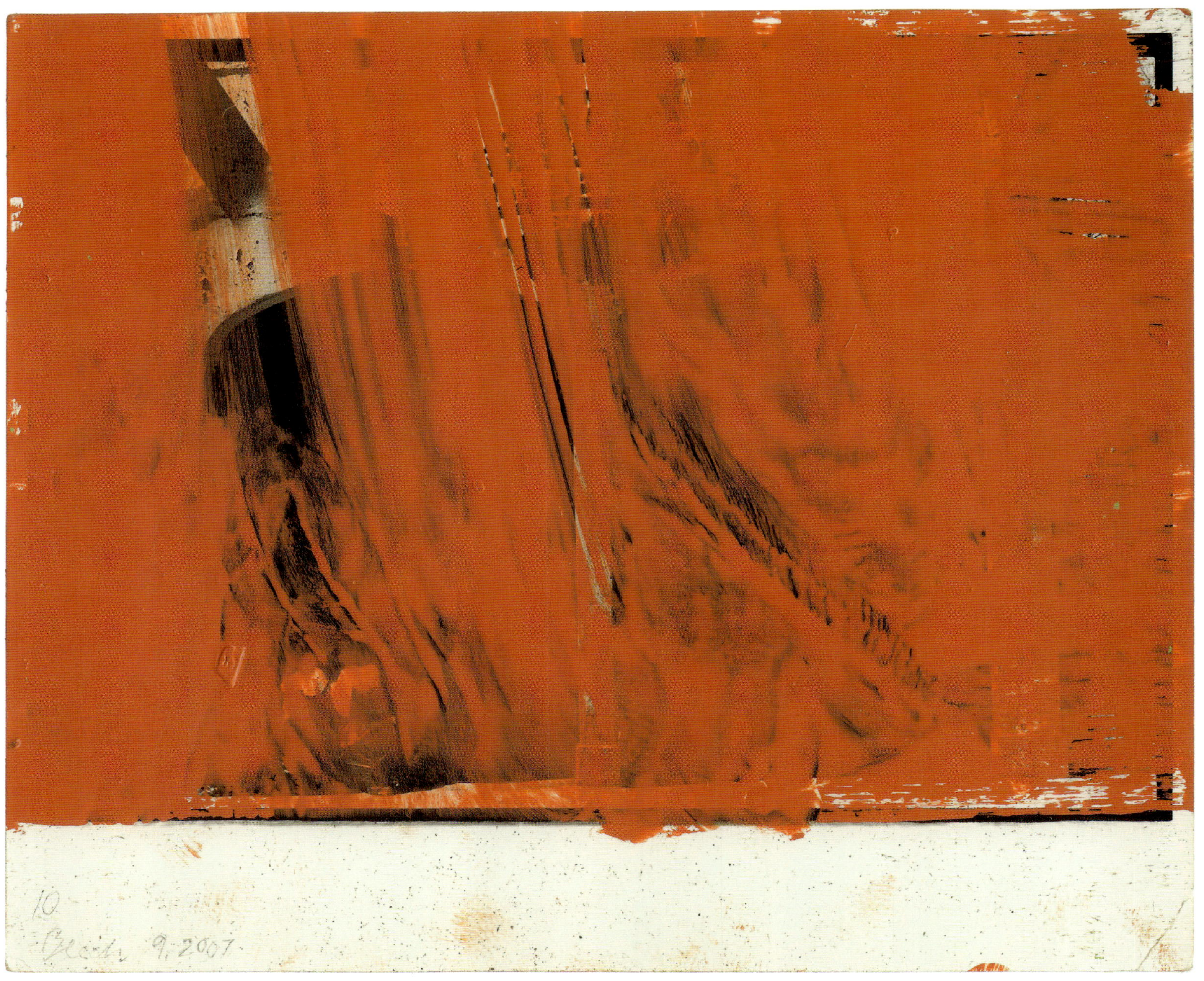

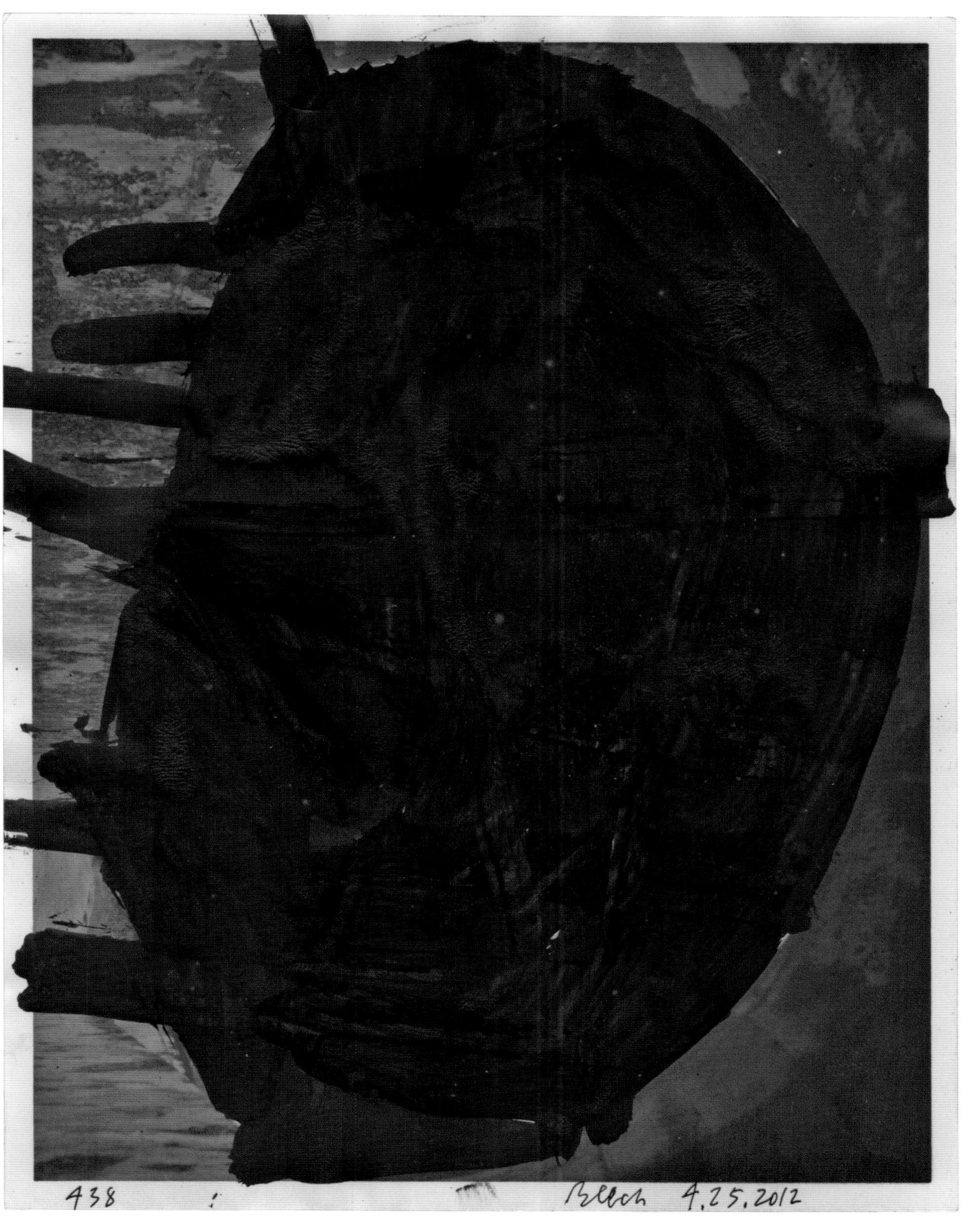
438
Black 4.25.2012

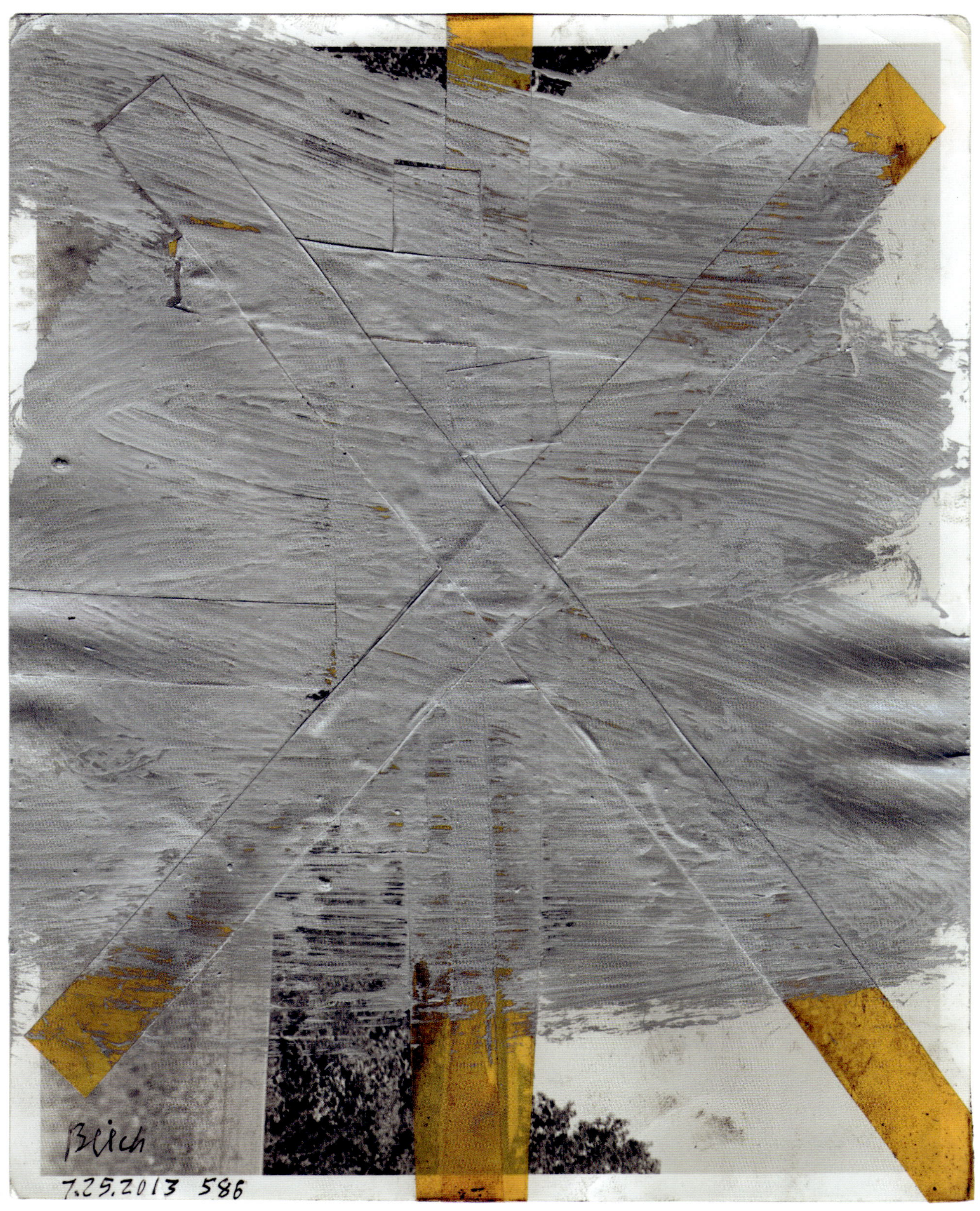
Beich
7.25.2013 586

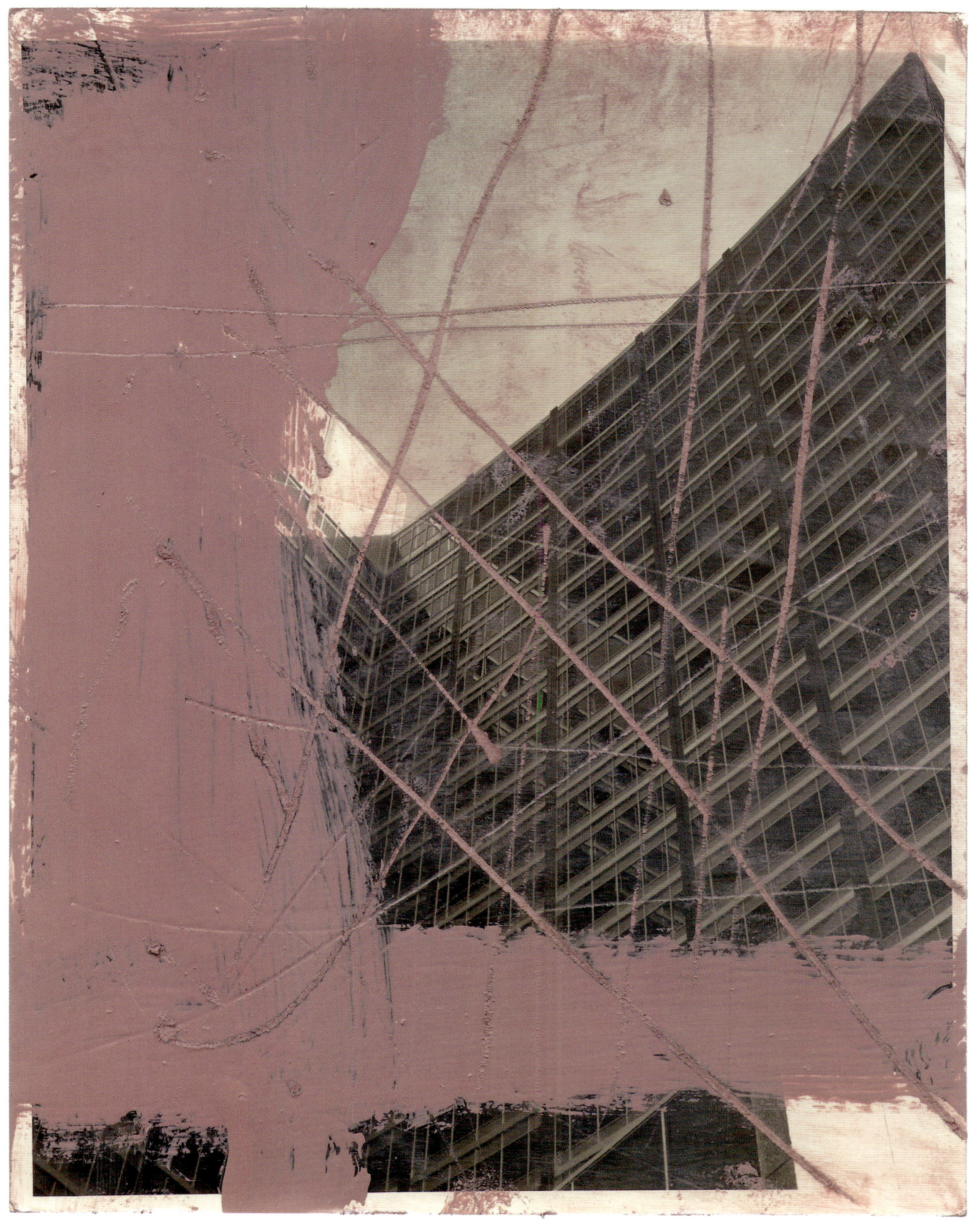

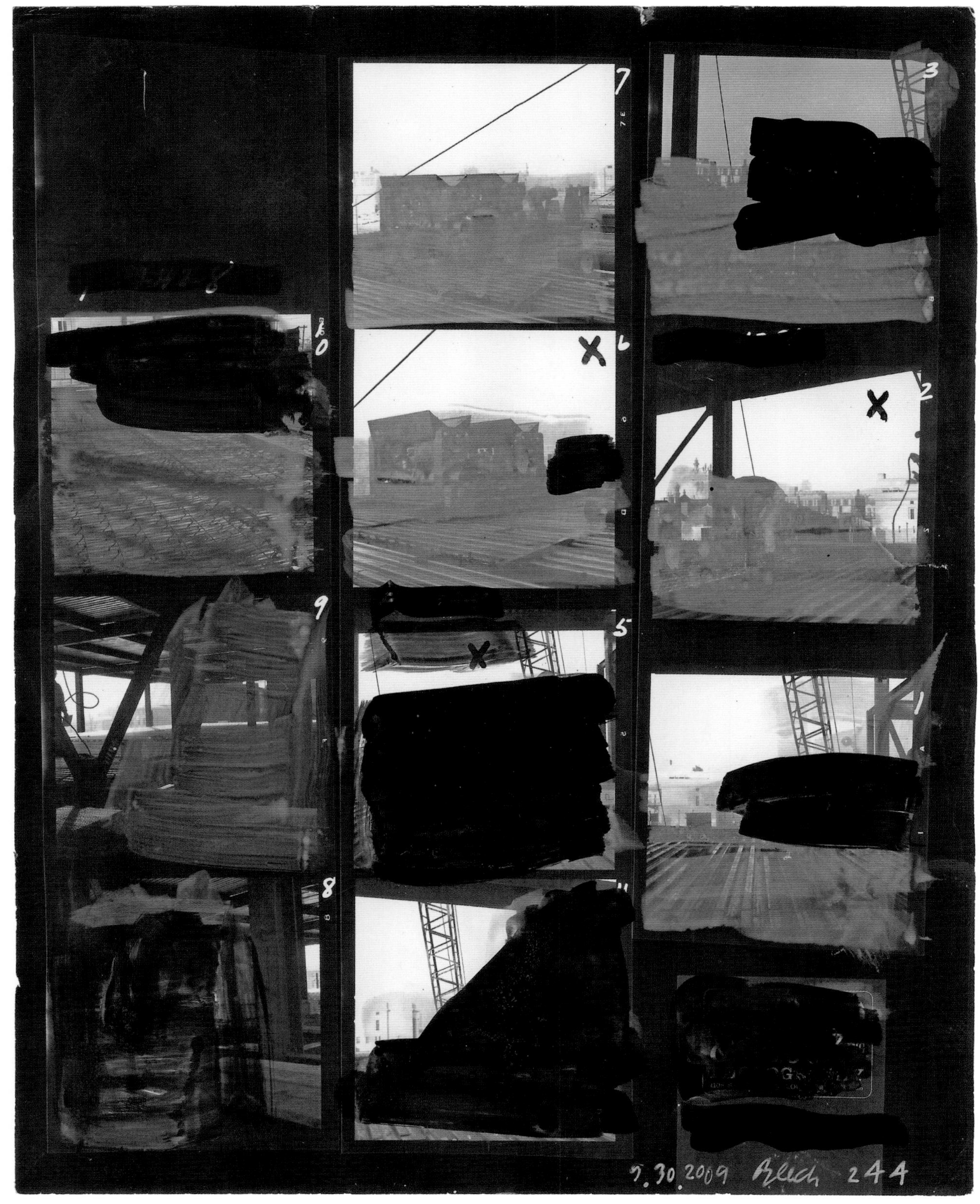
7.30.2009 Bleich 244

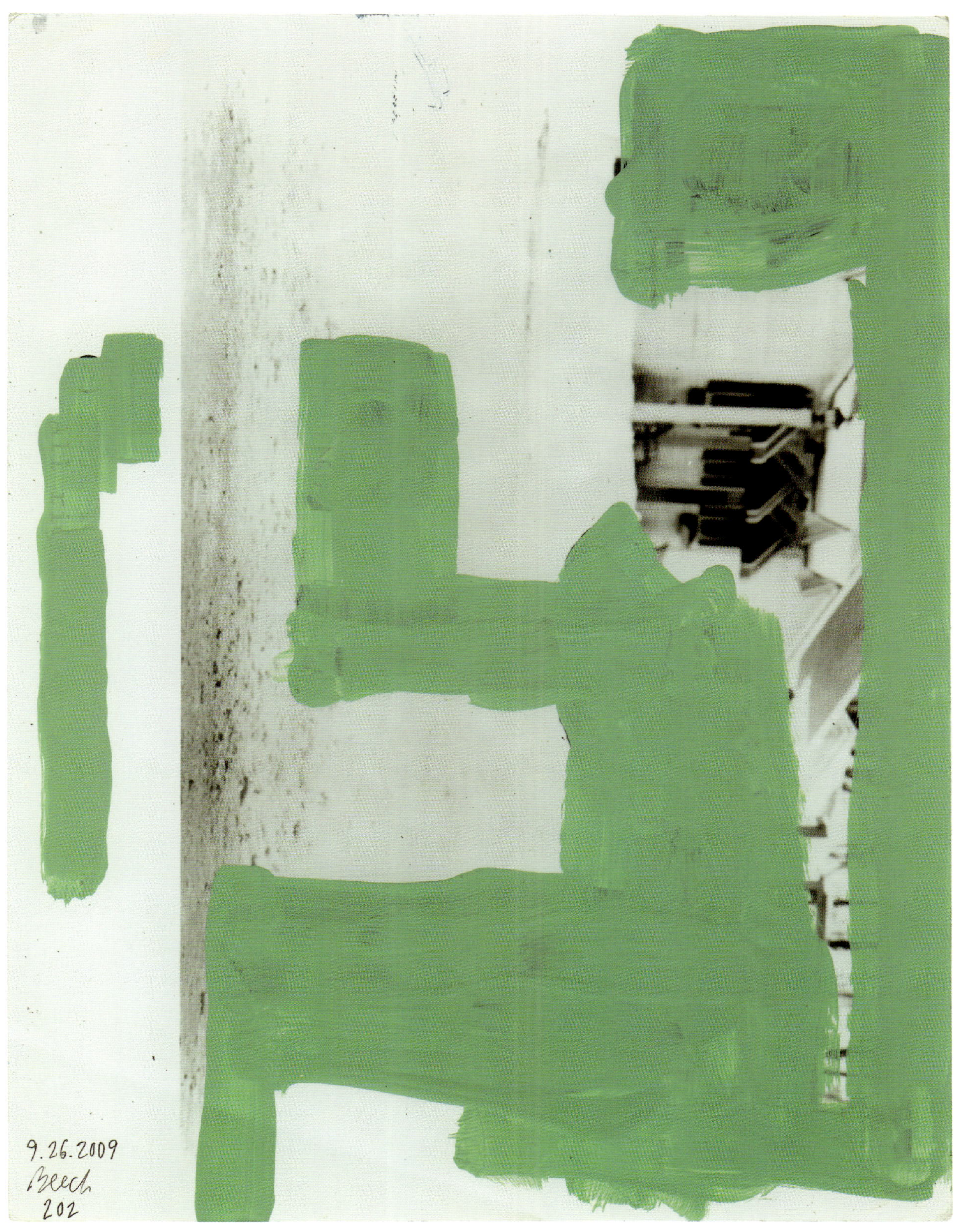
9.26.2009
Beech
202

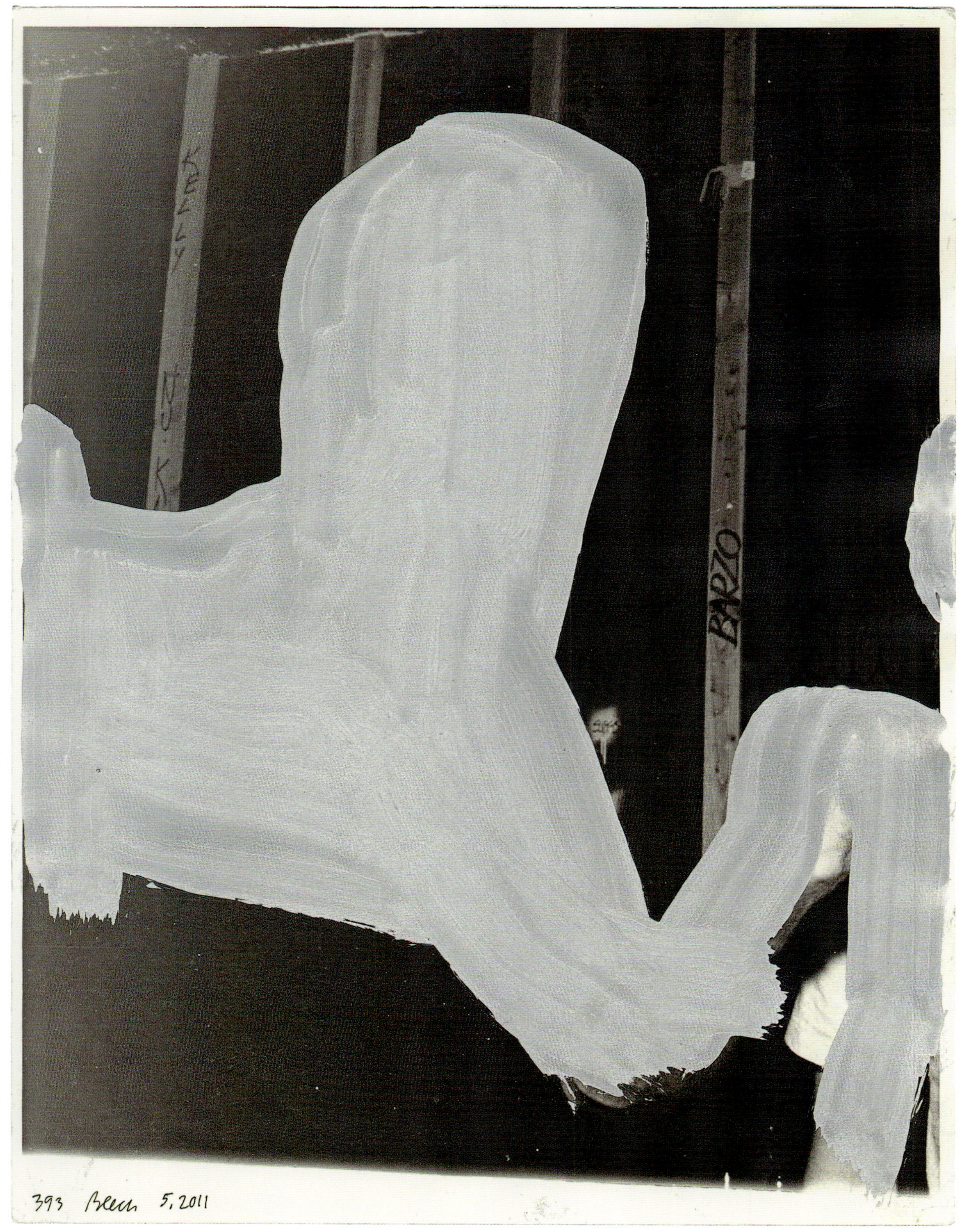

393 Beech 5.2011

2 Blech 9. 2007

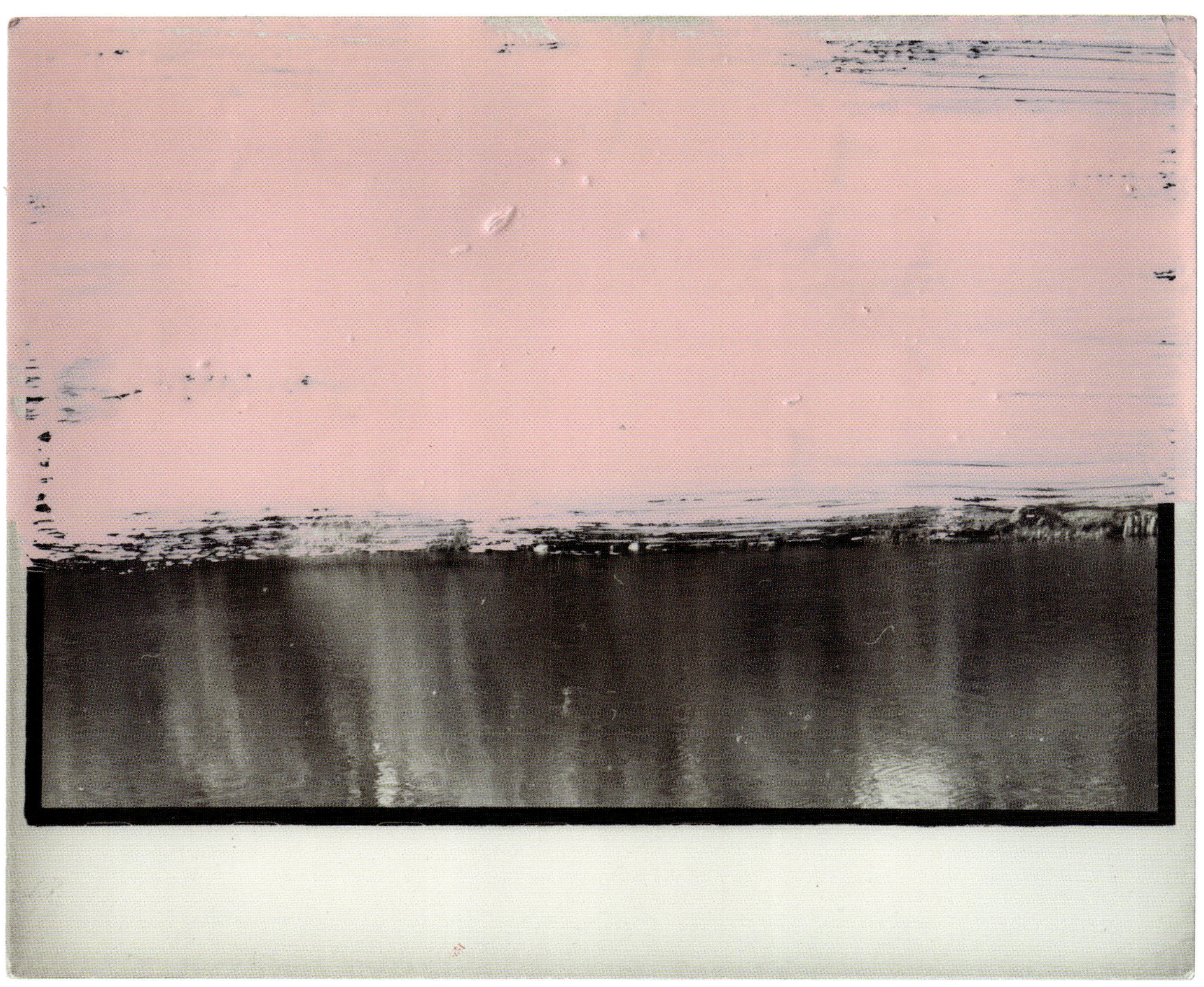

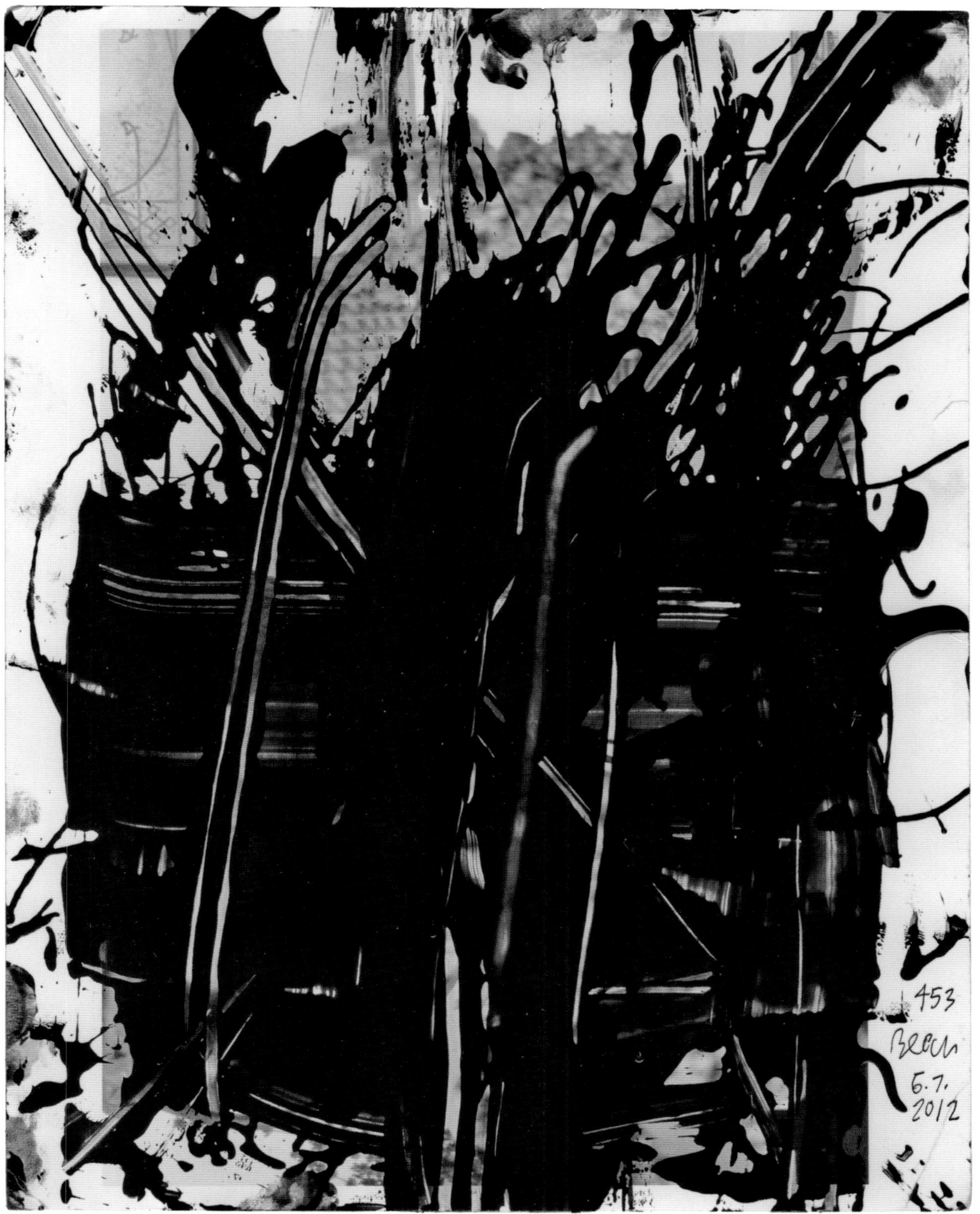

453
Beck
6.7.
2012

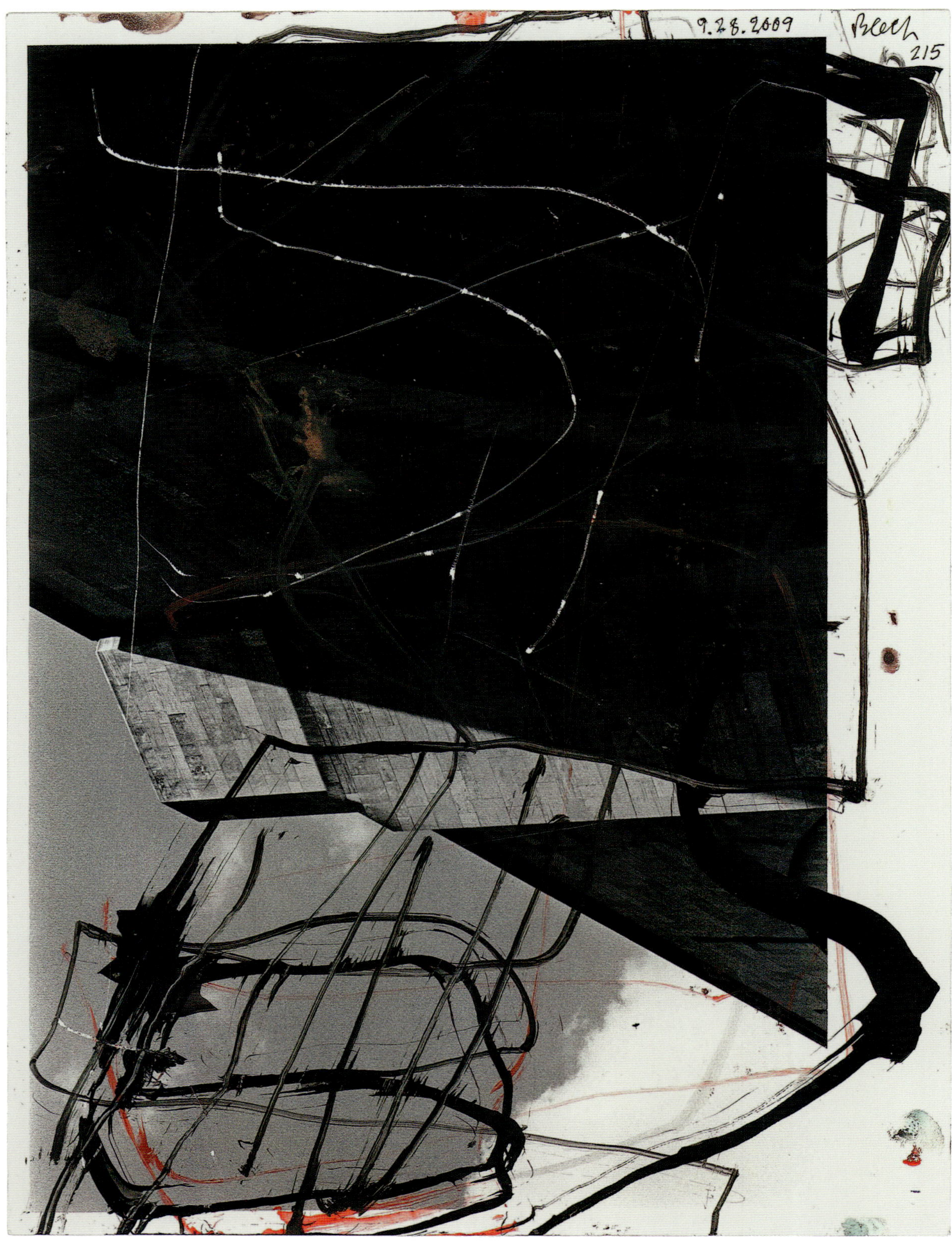

9.28.2009
Blech
215

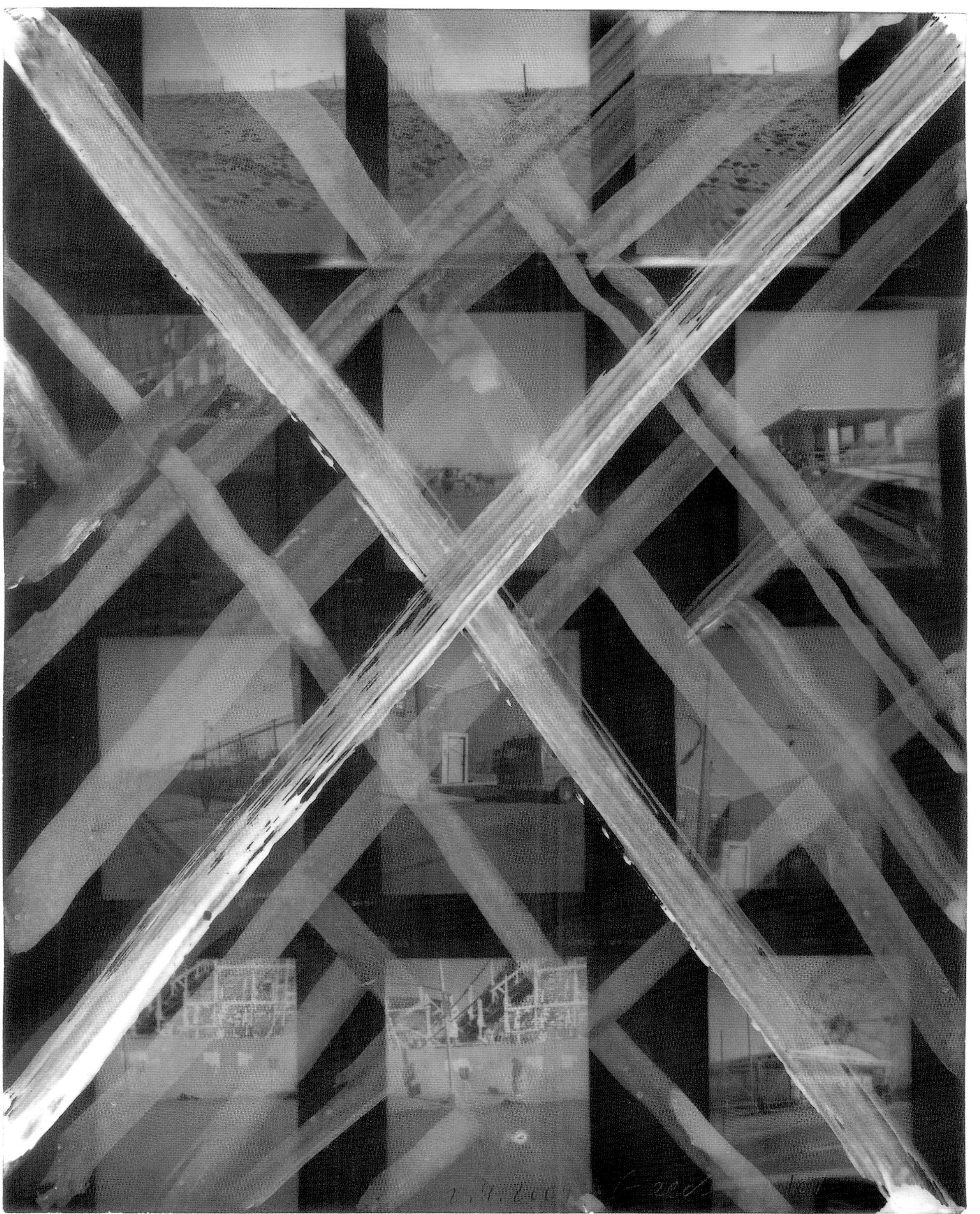

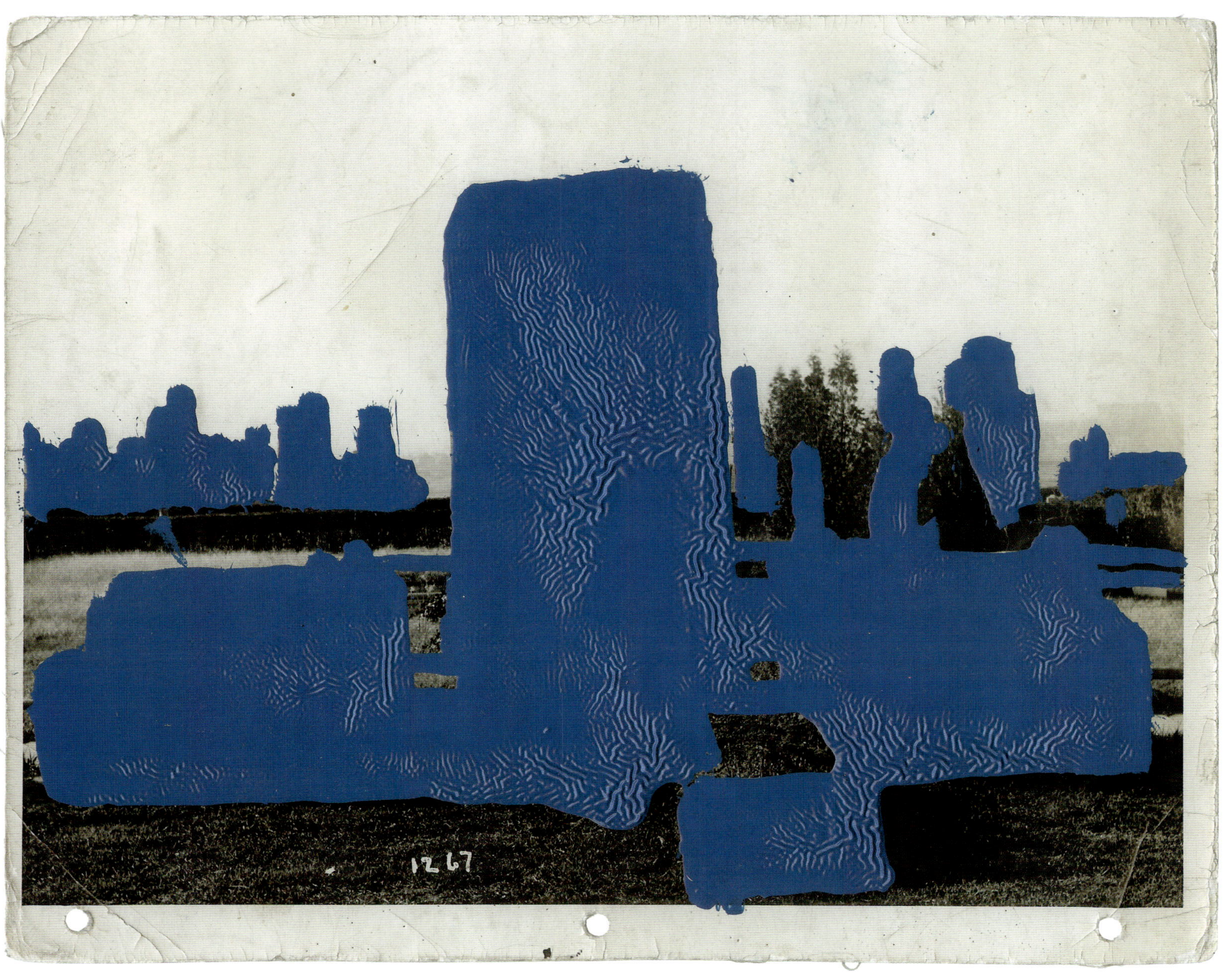
1267

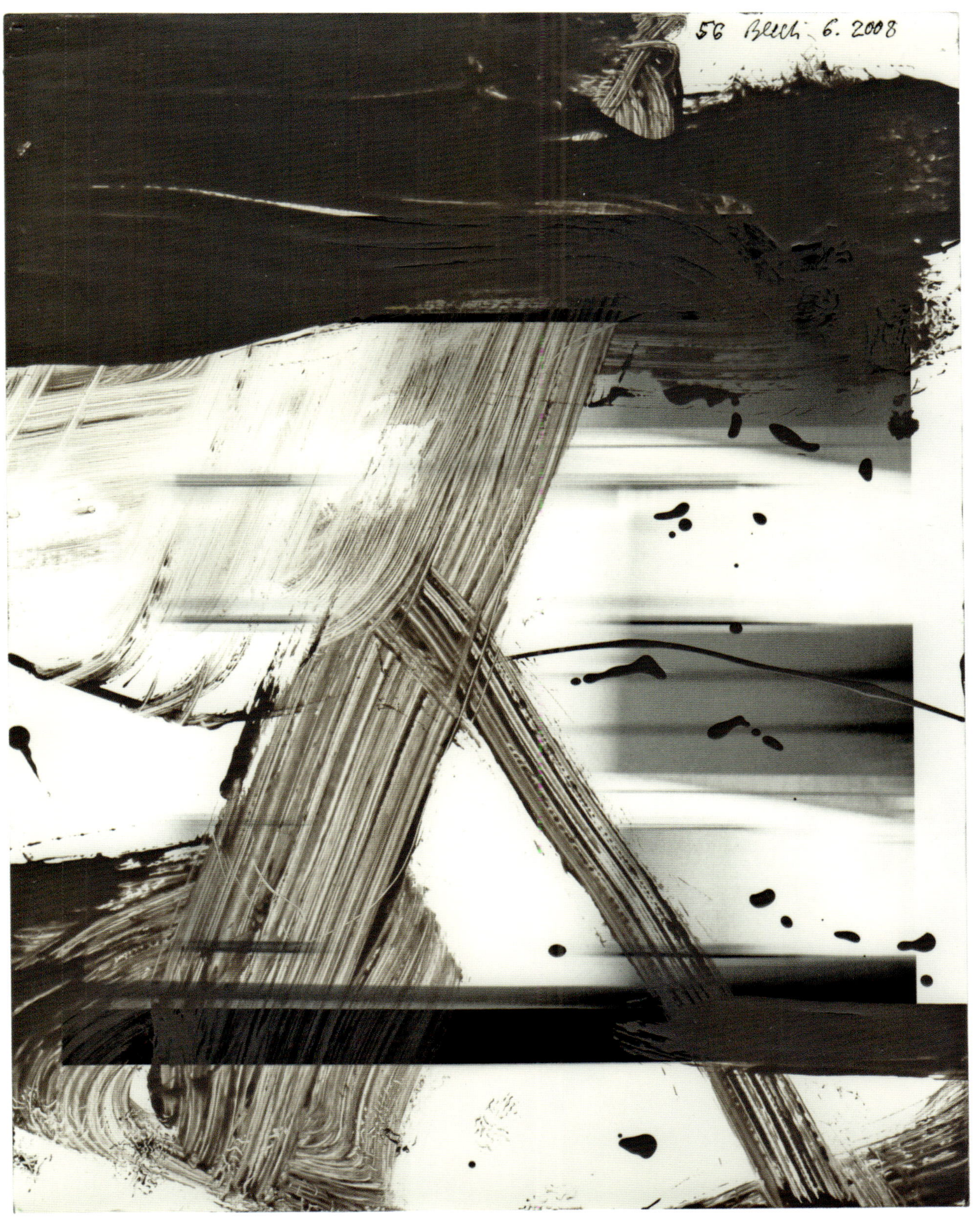
56 Bleck 6. 2008

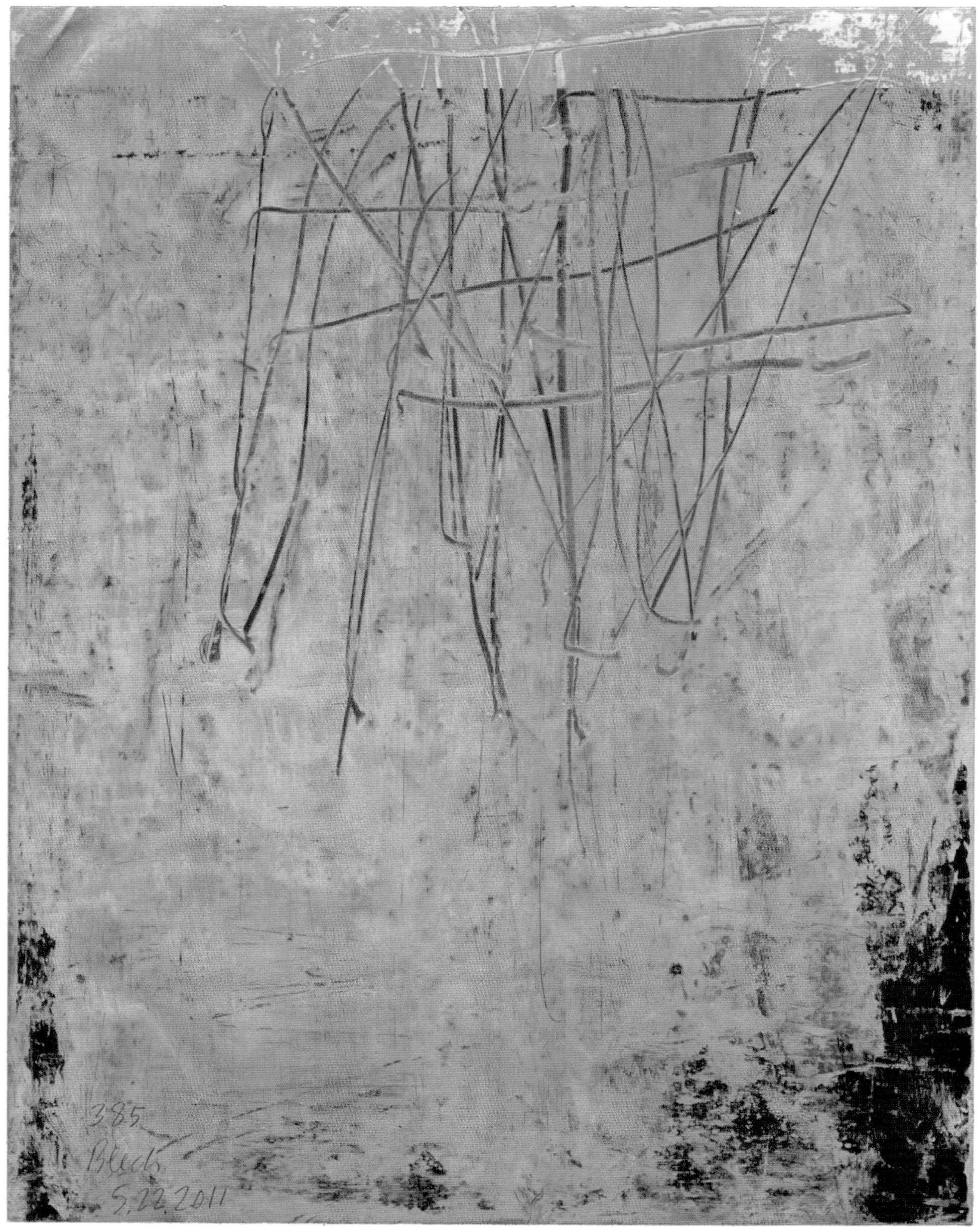
385
Bleck
5.22.2011

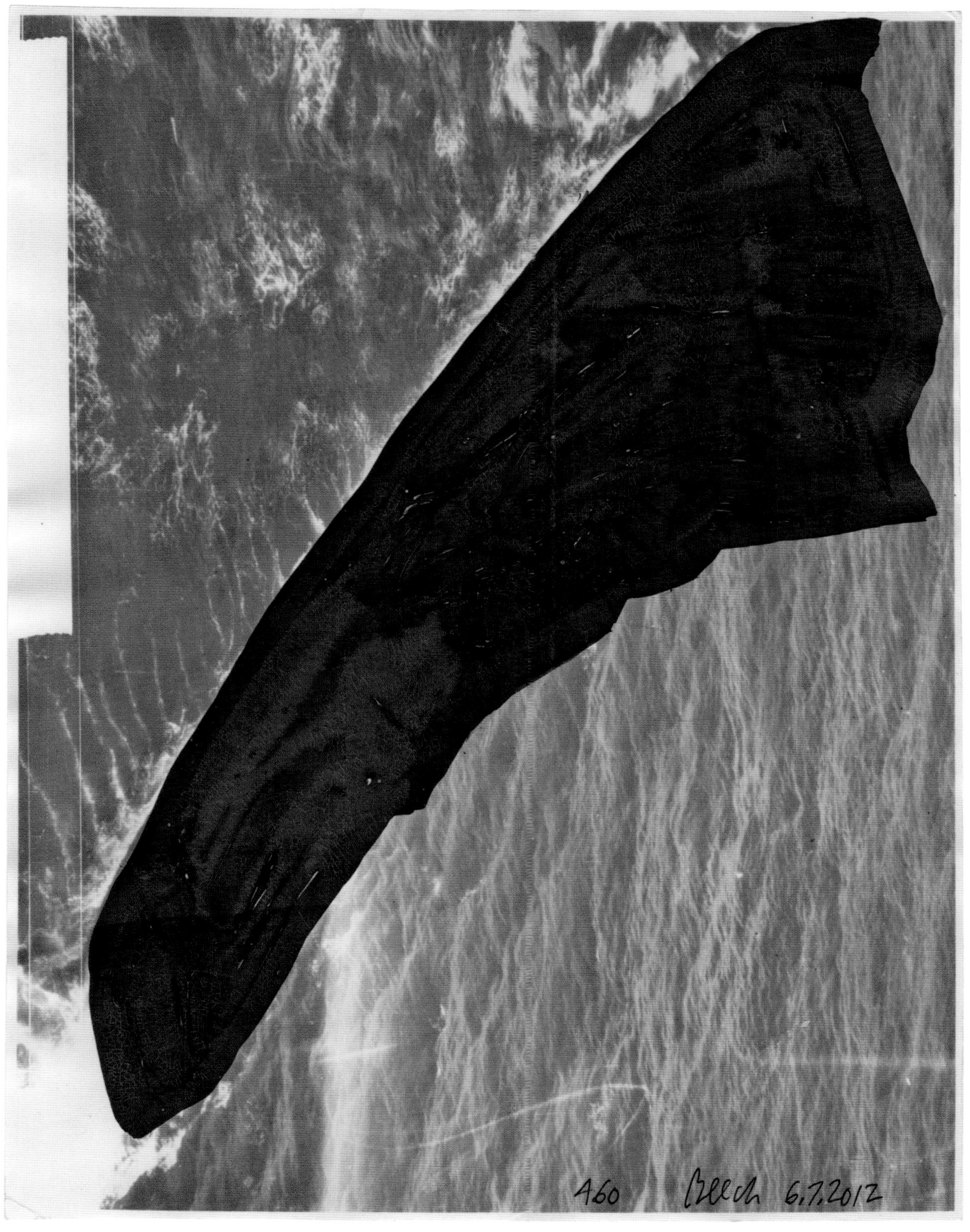

460 Blech 6.7.2012

7.21.2012
Beech   497

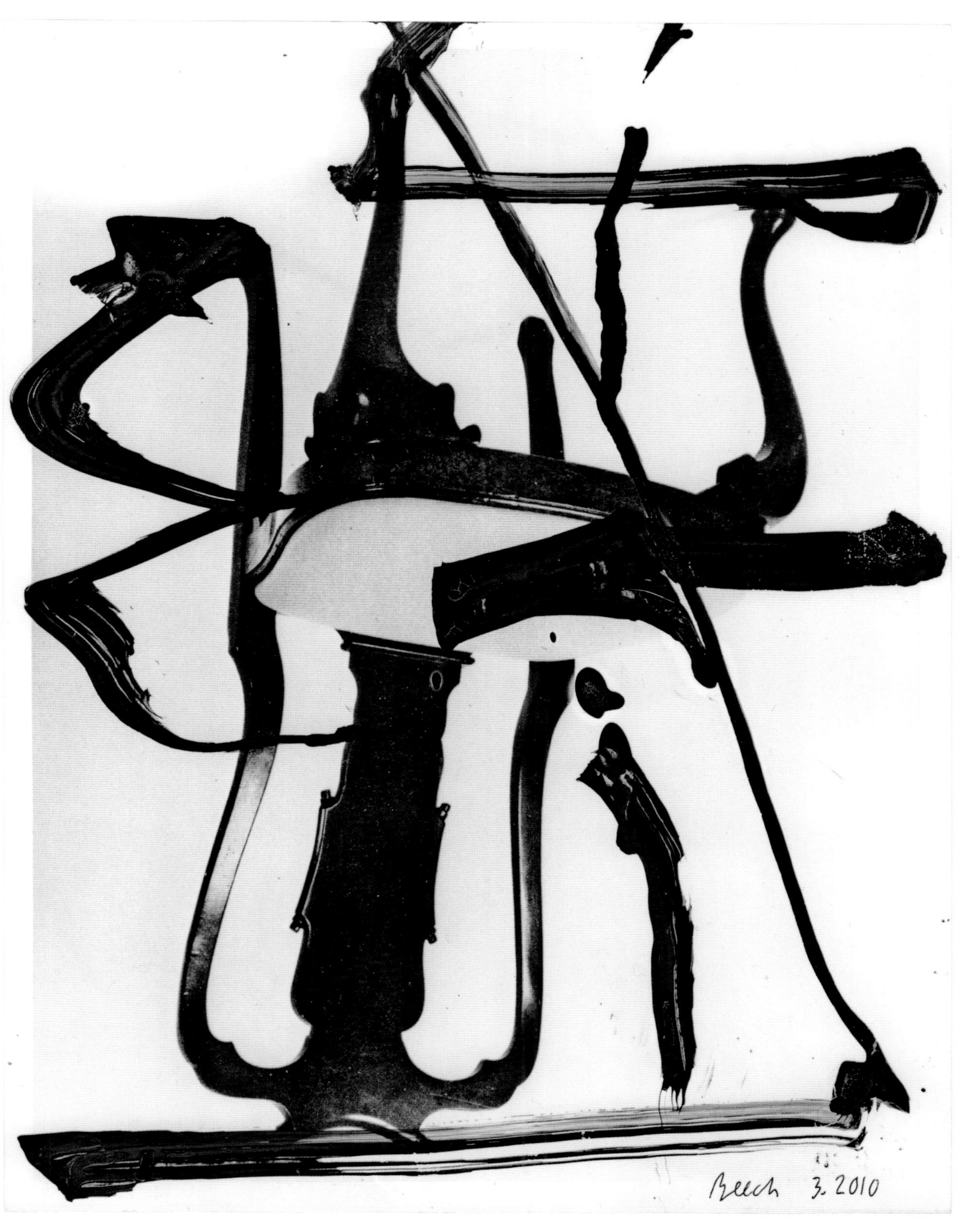

Beech 3. 2010

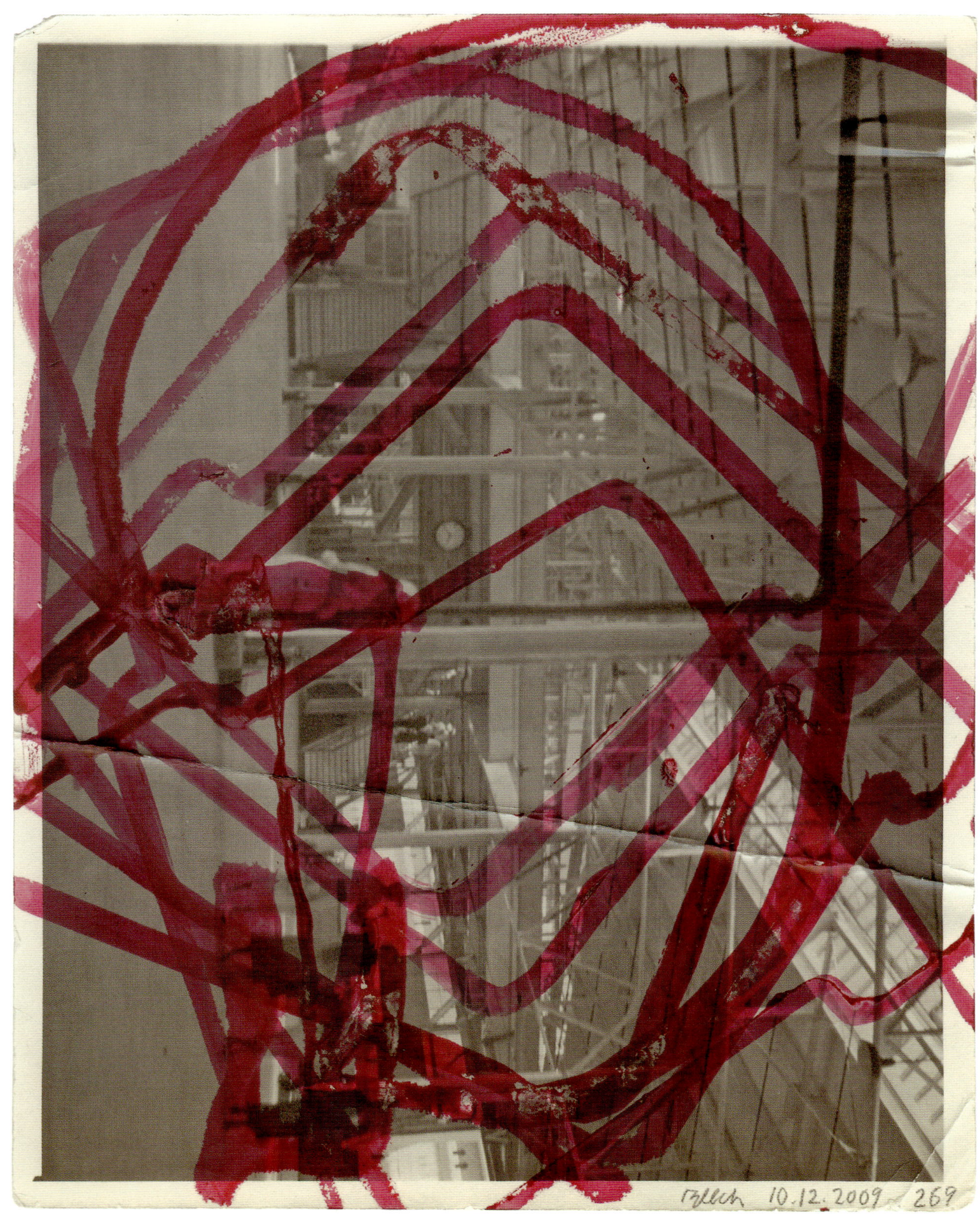
Blech 10.12.2009 269

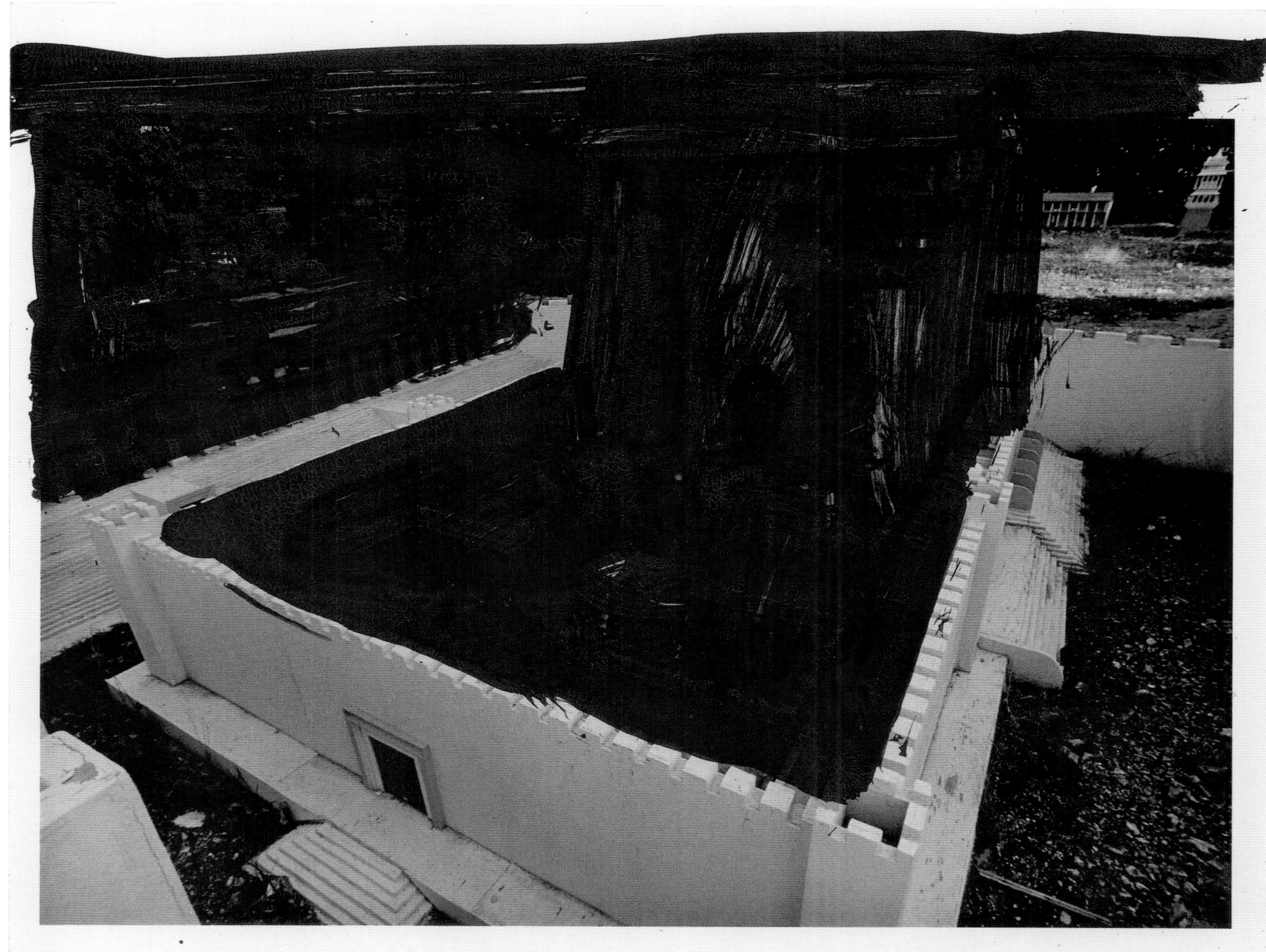

420   Beech   4.25.2012

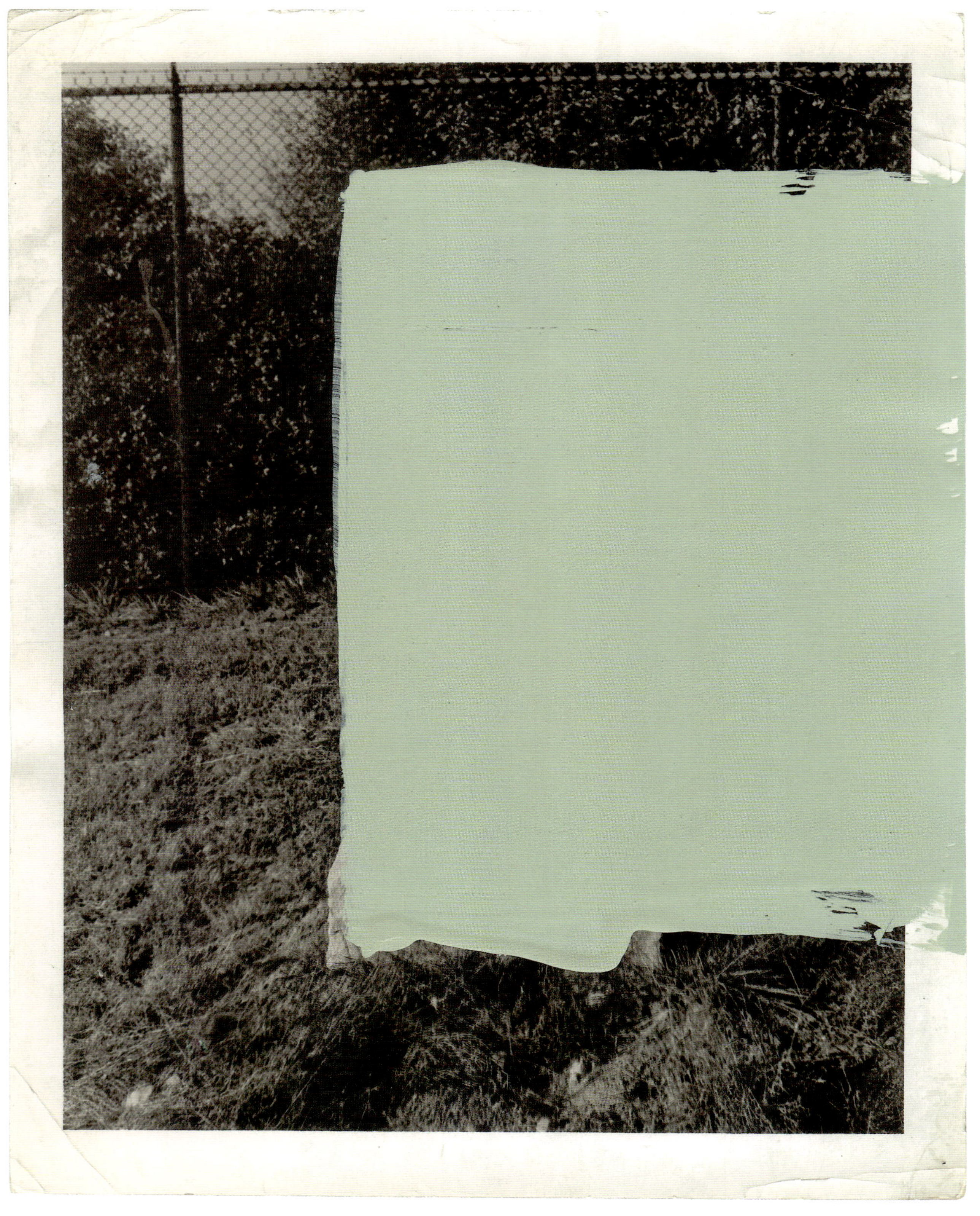

List of Works

Page 07
Found-Photo Drawing # 40, 2007
Enamel on Silver Gelatin Print, 10 x 8.125 inches

Page 08
Found-Photo Drawing # 271, 2009
Ink on Silver Gelatin Print, 11 x 8.625 inches

Page 09
Found-Photo Drawing # 410, 2011
Acrylic on Silver Gelatin Print, 8 x 10 inches

Page 10
Found-Photo Drawing (Monument Series # 187), 2009
Glow Enamel on Silver Gelatin Print, 9.875 x 8 inches

Page 11
Found-Photo Drawing # 187, 2009
Ink on Contact Sheet, 11 x 8.5 inches

Page 12
Found-Photo Drawing # 490, 2012
Pencil on Proof Photograph, 10 x 8 inches

Page 13
Found-Photo Drawing # 468, 2012
Ink on Silver Gelatin Print, 9.825 x 8 inches

Page 14
Found-Photo Drawing # 454, 2012
Enamel on Silver Gelatin Print, 10 x 8.125 inches

Page 15
Found-Photo Drawing # 284, 2009
Acrylic and Ballpoint Pen on Silver Gelatin Print, 10 x 8 inches

Page 16
Found-Photo Drawing # 245, 2009
Ink and China Marker on Silver Gelatin Print, 8.125 x 10 inches

Page 17
Found-Photo Drawing # 140, 2009
Enamel and Pencil on Silver Gelatin Print, 10 x 8 inches

Page 18
Found-Photo Drawing # 266, 2009
Ink and Acrylic on Silver Gelatin Print, 10 x 8 inches

Page 19
Found-Photo Drawing # 442, 2012
Acrylic on Silver Gelatin Print, 8 x 10 inches

Page 20
Found-Photo Drawing # 193, 2009
Enamel and Marker Pen on Silver Gelatin Print, 13.875 x 11 inches

Page 21
Found-Photo Drawing # 472, 2012
Enamel on Silver Gelatin Print, 8.125 x 9.875 inches

Page 22
Found-Photo Drawing # 231, 2009
Ink on Silver Gelatin Print, 10 x 8 inches

Page 23
Found-Photo Drawing # 340, 2010
Ink on Silver Gelatin Print, 8 x 10 inches

Page 24
Found-Photo Drawing # 503, 2012
Enamel on Silver Gelatin Print, 10 x 8 inches

Page 25
Found-Photo Drawing # 357, 2010
Ink on Silver Gelatin Print, 10 x 8 inches

Page 26
Found-Photo Drawing # 41, 2007
Enamel on Silver Gelatin Print, 9.875 x 7.875 inches

Page 27
Found-Photo Drawing # 587, 2013
Duct Tape on Silver Gelatin Print, 8.125 x 10 inches

Page 28
Found-Photo Drawing # 435, 2012
Ink on Silver Gelatin Print, 9.875 x 8.125 inches

Page 29
Found-Photo Drawing # 292, 2009
Ink and Acrylic on Silver Gelatin Print, 10 x 8.125 inches

Page 30
Found-Photo Drawing # 265, 2009
Acrylic on Silver Gelatin Print, 10 x 8 inches

Page 31
Found-Photo Drawing # 440 (Homage to Helen Levitt), 2012
Acrylic on Silver Gelatin Print, 10 x 8 inches

Page 32
Found-Photo Drawing # 492, 2012
Ink on Silver Gelatin Print, 8 x 10 inches

Page 33
Found-Photo Drawing # 203, 2009
Acrylic, Ink, and Marker Pen on Silver Gelatin Print, 10 x 8 inches

Page 34
Found-Photo Drawing # 321, 2009
Ink on Silver Gelatin Print, 11.125 x 8.5 inches

Page 35
Found-Photo Drawing # 142, 2009
Acrylic on Silver Gelatin Print 8.125 x 10 inches

Page 36
Found-Photo Drawing # 42, 2008
Aluminum Enamel and Pencil on Silver Gelatin Print, 10 x 8 inches

Page 37
Found-Photo Drawing # 39, 2007
Enamel on Silver Gelatin Print, 10 x 8 inches

Page 38
Found-Photo Drawing # 374, 2011
Ink on Silver Gelatin Print, 13.375 x 11 inches

Page 39
Found-Photo Drawing # 277, 2009
Acrylic and Ink on Silver Gelatin Print, 11 x 8.5 inches

Page 40
Found-Photo Drawing (Monument Series # 39), 2008
Enamel on Silver Gelatin Print, 10 x 8 inches

Page 41
Found-Photo Drawing # 516, 2013
Ink on Silver Gelatin Print, 8.625 x 10 inches

Page 42
Found-Photo Drawing # 568, 2013
Ink on Silver Gelatin Print, 8 x 10 inches

Page 43
Found-Photo Drawing # 151, 2009
Ink on Silver Gelatin Print, 11 x 8.625 inches

Page 44
Found-Photo Drawing # 81, 2009
Ink and Marker Pen on Silver Gelatin Print, 10 x 8 inches

Page 45
Found-Photo Drawing # 212, 2009
Ink on Color Kodak Print, 10 x 8 inches

Page 46
Found-Photo Drawing # 473-A, 2012
Ink on Silver Gelatin Print, 10 x 8 inches

Page 47
Found-Photo Drawing # 329, 2009
Ink on Contact Sheet, 11 x 8.5 inches

Page 48
Found-Photo Drawing # 334, 2010
Enamel on Silver Gelatin Print, 10 x 8 inches

Page 49
Found-Photo Drawing # 95, 2009
Acrylic and Pencil on Silver Gelatin Print, 10 x 8 inches

Page 50
Found-Photo Drawing # 433, 2012
Ink on Silver Gelatin Print, 9.875 x 8 inches

Page 51
Found-Photo Drawing (Monument Series # 182), 2009
Enamel on Silver Gelatin Print, 9.875 x 8 inches

Page 52
Found-Photo Drawing # 226, 2009
Ink on Color Kodak Print, 10 x 8 inches

Page 53
Found-Photo Drawing # 531, 2013
Ink on Silver Gelatin Print, 10 x 8 inches

Page 54
Found-Photo Drawing # 246, 2009
Acrylic on Silver Gelatin Print, 11 x 8.5 inches

Page 55
Found-Photo Drawing # 35, 2008
Enamel on Silver Gelatin Print, 8 x 10 inches

Page 56
Found-Photo Drawing (Monument Series # 144), 2009
Enamel on Silver Gelatin Print, 9.875 x 8 inches

Page 57
Found-Photo Drawing # 177, 2009
Aluminum Enamel, Marker Pen, Ink, and Color Pencil
on Silver Gelatin Print, 10 x 8 inches

Page 58
Found-Photo Drawing # 467, 2012
Enamel and Ink on Silver Gelatin Print, 10 x 8 inches

Page 59
Found-Photo Drawing # 300, 2009
Acrylic on Silver Gelatin Print, 8.125 x 10 inches

Page 60
Found-Photo Drawing # 588, 203
Ink on Color Contact Sheet, 10 x 8.125 inches

Page 61
Found-Photo Drawing # 132, 2009
Acrylic on Silver Gelatin Print, 10 x 8 inches

Page 62
Found-Photo Drawing # 570, 2013
Ink on Silver Gelatin Print, 8 x 10 inches

Page 63
Found-Photo Drawing # 327, 2009
Flashe Vinyl Paint on Contact Sheet, 10 x 8 inches

Page 64
Found-Photo Drawing # 234, 2009
Ink and Pencil on Silver Gelatin Print, 10 x 8 inches

Page 65
Found-Photo Drawing # 310, 2009
Enamel on Silver Gelatin Print, 13.875 x 11 inches

Page 66
Found-Photo Drawing # 493, 2012
Ink on Silver Gelatin Print, 10 x 8.5 inches

Page 67
Found-Photo Drawing # 3, 2007
Enamel and Pencil on Silver Gelatin Print, 8 x 10 inches

Page 68
Found-Photo Drawing # 159, 2009
Ink on Silver Gelatin Print, 8.125 x 10 inches

Page 69
Found-Photo Drawing # 160, 2009
Ink on Silver Gelatin Print, 8.125 x 10 inches

Page 70
Found-Photo Drawing # 317, 2009
Ink and Acrylic on Silver Gelatin Print, 10 x 8 inches

Page 71
Found-Photo Drawing # 33A, 2008
Aluminum Enamel on Silver Gelatin Print, 10 x 8 inches

Page 72
Found-Photo Drawing # 447, 2012
Flashe Vinyl Paint on Contact Sheet, 10 x 8 inches

Page 73
Found-Photo Drawing # 561, 2013
Flashe Vinyl Paint on Silver Gelatin Print, 10 x 8 inches

Page 74
Found-Photo Drawing # 196, 2009
Ink on Silver Gelatin Print, 10 x 8 inches

Page 75
Found-Photo Drawing # 200, 2009
Ink on Color Kodak Print, 10 x 8 inches

Page 76
Found-Photo Drawing # 499, 2012
Enamel and Pencil on Silver Gelatin Print, 10 x 8 inches

Page 77
Found-Photo Drawing # 491, 2012
Ink on Silver Gelatin Print, 8.875 x 8.125 inches

Page 78
Found-Photo Drawing # 10, 2007
Enamel on Silver Gelatin Print, 8 x 10 inches

Page 79
Found-Photo Drawing # 438, 2012
Ink on Silver Gelatin Print, 9.875 x 8 inches

Page 80
Found-Photo Drawing # 586, 2013
Aluminum Enamel, Electrical Tape on Silver Gelatin Print,
10 x 8.125 inches

Page 81
Found-Photo Drawing # 29, 2008
Enamel on Silver Gelatin Print, 10 x 8 inches

Page 82
Found-Photo Drawing # 244, 2009
Ink on Marked Contact Sheet, 10 x 8.125 inches

Page 83
Found-Photo Drawing # 202, 2009
Acrylic on Silver Gelatin Print, 10 x 7.875 inches

Page 84
Found-Photo Drawing # 393, 2011
Aluminum Enamel on Silver Gelatin Print, 14 x 11 inches

Page 85
Found-Photo Drawing # 2, 2007
Enamel on Silver Gelatin Print, 8 x 10 inches

Page 86, Jacket Cover
Found-Photo Drawing (Water Series # 4), 2008
Enamel on Silver Gelatin Print, 8 x 10 inches

Page 87
Found-Photo Drawing # 453, 2012
Enamel on Silver Gelatin Print, 9.875 x 8 inches

Page 88
Found-Photo Drawing # 215, 2009
Ink on Silver Gelatin Print, 10.875 x 8.5 inches

Page 89
Found-Photo Drawing # 107, 2009
Ink and Pencil on Contact Sheet, 9.875 x 8 inches

Page 90
Found-Photo Drawing (Monument Series # 188), 2009
Enamel on Silver Gelatin Print, 7.75 x 10 inches

Page 91
Found-Photo Drawing # 56, 2008
Enamel on Silver Gelatin Print, 10 x 8 inches

Page 92
Found-Photo Drawing # 385, 2011
Aluminum Enamel and Pencil on Silver Gelatin Print, 10 x 8 inches

Page 93
Found-Photo Drawing # 460, 2012
Ink on Silver Gelatin Print, 9.75 x 7.75 inches

Page 94
Found-Photo Drawing # 497, 2012
Enamel on Silver Gelatin Print, 10 x 8 inches

Page 95
Found-Photo Drawing (Chair Series # 7), 2010
Ink on Silver Gelatin Print, 10 x 8 inches

Page 96
Found-Photo Drawing # 269, 2009
Ink on Silver Gelatin Print, 9.875 x 8 inches

Page 97
Found-Photo Drawing # 420, 2012
Ink on Silver Gelatin Print, 8 x 10 inches

Page 98
Found-Photo Drawing (Monument Series # 77), 2008
Enamel on Silver Gelatin Print, 9.875 x 8 inches

Bridged Field
Found-Photo Drawings

Drawings © 2014 John Beech
Foreword © 2014 Alexander Nagel

Published in the United States by powerHouse Books,
a division of powerHouse Cultural Entertainment, Inc.
37 Main Street, Brooklyn, NY 11201-1021
telephone 212.604.9074, fax 212.366.5247
e-mail: info@powerHouseBooks.com, website: www.powerHouseBooks.com

First edition, 2014

Library of Congress Control Number: 2013955765

ISBN 978-1-57687-691-6

Book design by Kiki Bauer

Color separations by Embassy Graphics, Canada
Printed and bound in China through Asia Pacific Offset

www.johnbeech.com

10 9 8 7 6 5 4 3 2 1